My 33 Years

INSIDE
THE HOUSE OF
CASH

My 33 Years

INSIDE
THE HOUSE OF
CASH

A Special Tribute to My Closest Friends:
Johnny, June, and Mother Maybelle

Peggy Knight

PREMIUM PRESS AMERICA
NASHVILLE, TENNESSEE

My 33 Years Inside the House of Cash
By Peggy Knight

Published by PREMIUM PRESS AMERICA

ISBN 1-887654-92-5
Library of Congress Catalog Number 2004105841

PREMIUM PRESS AMERICA gift books are available at special discounts for premiums, sales promotions, fund-raising, or educational use. For details contact the Publisher at P.O. Box 159015, Nashville, TN 37215, or phone toll free (800) 891-7323 or (615) 256-8484, or fax (615) 256-8624.

www.premiumpressamerica.com

Design by Armour&Armour, Nashville, Tennessee
Cover design by Barry Edwards

First Edition 2004

1 2 3 4 5 6 7 8 9 10

To all the fans of my closest friends:

Johnny Cash, June Carter Cash,

and Mother Maybelle

Contents

Foreword by Jo Walker-Meador

IN THIS BOOK, you will see the real Mother Maybelle, the real June Carter, and the real Johnny Cash. *Inside the House of Cash* is written in an easily read and enjoyable style by Peggy Knight, who spent more than thirty years living with and working for these three wonderful people.

I met Johnny and June in Montgomery, Alabama, in October of 1964. I was waiting for them curbside at the hotel when they roared up in a fancy convertible, looking like a million dollars and evidently very much in love. They came to Montgomery for the world premiere of the Hank Williams movie, *Your Cheatin' Heart.* They performed there for the Country Music Association, the sponsor and benefactor of the premiere.

I had met Johnny briefly at the Coliseum in Louisville, Kentucky, in March of 1959 when he and the Tennessee Two played a benefit show for CMA. Johnny not only performed gratis, but he also bore the expense of flying himself and the band up from Shreveport, Louisiana, where they had played the Louisiana Hayride the previous night.

One morning in the early '60s when I unlocked the door to our little CMA office, I found a note written on the back of a blank counter check that read "Anytime I can do something for CMA, let me know," signed Johnny Cash. Through the years, he lived up to that promise.

I was privileged to be in their home on many different occasions–for lunch and for one of June's sales, for celebrations under the big tent on the tennis courts, and for guitar pulls. Those guitar pulls were the most fun. Johnny and June were so wonderful to help struggling songwriters. In this book, Peggy tells about the many people the Cashes helped on their way to success.

There is no way to convey the great musical legacy these three left the world. If you asked the question, literally around the world, "Do you know the name of anyone in country music?" the answer would be *Johnny Cash*. Recently, a gentleman pledged more than half a million dollars to purchase Mother Maybelle's guitar for permanent display at the Country Music Hall of Fame and Museum. The talent and music of these three people will be enjoyed worldwide down through the ages.

Peggy Knight's book reveals over and over the warmth, the caring spirit, and the utmost generosity of these three, as well as the down-to-earth lovable people whose fame never superseded these wonderful attributes.

Despite the success and fame they achieved, each had some real burdens to bear. They bore them well, kept their sense of humor, and made life wonderful for all those around them. They knew how to have fun.

You will enjoy the openness of these beloved people as told by Peggy Knight, who literally did everything for them and treasures her life with them.

Country Music Hall of Fame member Jo Walker-Meador was executive director of the Country Music Association from its founding in 1958 until 1992.

Preface

THIS IS MY tribute to Maybelle Carter, John Cash, and June Carter Cash.

I worked for them, traveled with them, and took care of them for thirty-three years. I saw my friends at their best and at their worst, during their greatest joy and in their darkest despair. But it's the good memories—the laughs, the good times, the very special people—that I cherish and want to share with you.

I'd need ten books to tell everything I know. John and June were both so much bigger than life, I could write a whole book on either of them and still not even scratch the surface.

I was incredibly lucky to see what they were really like off-stage and behind the scenes. In all my life, I've never met more down-to-earth, good-hearted people than Maybelle, John, and June. That's the story I want to tell.

Over thirty-plus years, details always grow hazy, and faces and places blur together. I've tried to be as accurate as I could about names and dates, but forgive me if I'm off by a year or get a name wrong. I'm especially indebted to my old friend Mark Stielper, Cash historian extraordinaire, for help with the details (and for sticking by me), and to my new friends Joan Armour, Jan Stinson, and Christopher Armour for helping me tell my story.

This book would not have been possible without the help of many other people as well:

Linda Lael Miller, a long-time friend and *New York Times* best-selling novelist, and her father Skip Lael always believed in me. Linda especially encouraged me to write about my life with the Carter and Cash families.

Johnny Ellis, my attorney, helped me find the right people who could make my dream of writing a book come true–Ray Throckmorton, the entire staff of Armour&Armour, and Bette and George Schnitzer.

My friends Dennis Devine, Pat Katz, P. Marsheck, Barbara Sather, and Kathy Tittle shared wonderful photographs from their personal collections.

My good friend Irene Gibbs nearly always had the answer to my many questions.

And Patti Martin, Anna Bisceglia, and Jay Davis are very special to me.

My heartfelt thanks to all of you.

This book is dedicated to the memory of my three closest friends. I'm telling the world what I know about the people I loved the most, so that you can love them even more.

Peggy Knight
September 2004

Bingo Ladies

BINGO CHANGED my life forever.

I walked into the VFW Club in Inglewood one night in 1967 to play some bingo. I would walk out of Johnny Cash's house for the last time thirty-six years later.

The woman with the bright blue eyes sitting across from me that night was Mother Maybelle Carter, the legend I'd listened to on the radio for years. I've always enjoyed talking to strangers, so I introduced myself and told her I was a big fan.

As we played, I chatted with her and her good friend Minnie, who was married to Grand Ole Opry star Hank Snow. And I talked her into buying a raffle ticket for a school fundraiser. I was helping a friend's granddaughter sell them; the top prize was a small cedar chest full of candy.

As we were getting ready to leave that night, Maybelle–she insisted from the beginning I call her that–asked me if I'd be coming back. I said I thought so.

As luck, or fate, would have it, Maybelle's raffle ticket was the winner. The next day I took the chest to her home on Due West Avenue in Madison, and stayed to drive her and Minnie (who lived just a few streets over) to the bingo hall.

That became our routine. More nights than not, you'd find us playing bingo from seven-thirty until the club closed at ten-thirty p.m.

We got together to play canasta and Rook. One night Maybelle invited me over for dinner. We had pheasant, a first for me. Maybelle's husband had killed it, and she plucked it and cooked it.

Minnie didn't drive, and Maybelle didn't like to, so I helped them out. That led to my first road trip. I drove Maybelle and Minnie down to New Port Richey, Florida, where Maybelle owned a big house with her husband, whom Maybelle called "Daddy." His given name was Ezra, but everybody called him "Eck."

Eck was kind of an odd bird.

Brother to A.P. Carter, who revolutionized country music in the Thirties, Eck couldn't play a note. He was a country boy, and didn't take a bath but once a week–and sometimes thought that was too much.

He'd applied for early retirement from the railroad in 1943 because of high blood pressure, and hadn't done much since but hunt and fish.

He loved fishing, but he didn't have much sense of direction. So he'd tie a ribbon to the riverbank where he launched his boat. Well, I reckon he didn't have much sense of time, either, and often it would be dark before he headed in. Except now he couldn't see his ribbon.

Many a night I'd get a call from Maybelle. "Come over and sit a while," she'd say. "Daddy's lost again." I'd pick up Minnie and we'd play cards in Maybelle's kitchen until Mr. Carter turned up.

Once in a while I'd stay all night until the Coast Guard tracked him down the next day.

I remember one time Mr. Carter managed to find his own way home with a big catch. He wanted to take a picture but didn't have anything to hang them on. Well, he

We played cards for hours at Maybelle's or Minnie's kitchen table.

poked around and came out with a crutch. Maybelle had one end and Minnie held the other while Mr. Carter hung those fish on the crutch and took a picture.

Maybelle used to say that Eck could spend money faster than she could make it. She'd get aggravated with him about the Sears bill. He was always buying things whether he needed them or not: After his death they found four or five fuseboxes in his basement.

One time Mr. Carter came back from a trip to Florida pulling a trailer behind his Mercedes. Maybelle asked him what he was going to do with it.

"I don't know," he said, "I'll have to pay for it first."

Well, Maybelle told him she wasn't buying him another thing. "That's all right, May," he said. "June will."

Minnie Snow and Maybelle display Eck's big catch on a crutch.

I snapped this picture of Maybelle and Eck visiting with a fan back stage at a concert. That's Minnie Snow in the background.

He parked it in the backyard and filled it with books. He loved to read, and the stacks of books soon reached the ceiling. Eventually he would sleep out there, books and papers covering the bed except for a narrow place on one side where he lay down.

Mr. Carter loved to put things on rollers: He put boxes, chairs, tables on rollers, and he even had a stump with wheels. Maybelle said he'd put her on wheels if he could.

Mr. Carter was a roamer. He spent most of his time in Virginia. He'd stay in Nashville for a while, then decide to take off for Florida or go back to Virginia.

* * *

I saw a lot of Maybelle, and one day I drove Maybelle over to visit her daughter June and her new husband, Johnny Cash.

I thought they were really cool. John was young and handsome. June was incredibly kind, and very pretty.

Mr. Carter started getting sick about 1971, and one day around then while Maybelle and I were at June's visiting, June asked me if I could help her mother take care of her dad. So I went to Maybelle's house every day for a year or so, doing the cooking and helping her take care of her husband. Starting in 1972, when he was in and out of the hospital ten times over the next three years, June asked me to stay the night with Maybelle.

Maybelle inscribed her album "Mother Maybelle Carter" for me.

Mr. Carter died in January 1975, and June gave me a call. Maybelle had told her, "Peggy's the only person I'd ever want to live with me." June said, "Honey, I know you're single and got your own life, but I wonder if you would consider living with Mama. We'd take care of you."

From that point on, I never went anywhere without Maybelle. I'd even take her with me when I visited my mother and sisters, or when I went to play cards with my brother. She told me more than once, "You mean the world to me." And she was always thanking me for taking care of her. She wrote on one of her albums "I sure am glad to have you live with me" and gave it to me.

I'd do anything for Maybelle. One night I heard her roaming around about three a.m. I went to check on her and she said she just kept thinking about her favorite sandwich: bacon, bell pepper, and sliced onion on a biscuit. I offered to make her one. "Oh, you don't have to do that," she told me, but I went downstairs, fried some bacon, and made fresh biscuits.

When I got back upstairs, she was lying in bed waiting. "I smelled the bacon cooking and knew what you were doing," she said.

For ten years, I lived in the house on Due West Avenue. Maybelle's brother Toob and his wife Babe moved in with us.

Right off the bat, Babe said, "You do the cooking 'cause I don't like it, and I'll do the dishes." Toob took care

I lived with Maybelle and her brother Toob.

of the sixteen acres, mowing the yard and bush-hogging the fields.

We put in a garden with corn, tomatoes, potatoes, beets, cucumbers, leaf lettuce, and green onions. Maybelle loved to can, and she taught me to put up beets, freeze corn, and make relish from the tomatoes.

We had a great time. Kinfolk were always coming to visit. We would play canasta or rummy 'til all hours. And we'd go on the road some with June and John. Maybelle would sing a couple of songs. Even when she didn't feel like singing on stage, she had a microphone behind the curtain so she could sing backup for Helen, June, and Anita.

Maybelle loved bowling about as much as bingo. We

even formed a team—the Rebel Housewives—and joined a league at the Madison Bowl. We were league champions three times. And I won the sportsmanship trophy four years in a row. Every year Maybelle asked me, "How come I can't win sportsmanship?"

She had a great sense of humor. We were visiting her friend Des Little, and he started teasing her about being dressed all in black like her son-in-law. "What we need to

The Rebel Housewives—Frances Merryman, Eve Ray, Maybelle, and I—won our bowling league championship three times.

Maybelle's friend Des Little dressed her up like a gunslinger.

do is make a cowgirl out of you," Des said. He rummaged up a cowboy hat, holster, and gun. Maybelle dressed up like a gunfighter and posed for a picture.

When she was recognized by the Smithsonian Institution, Maybelle held a press conference to talk about her music. She had a bandage on her middle finger, and held it up for everyone to see. "This is what you get from playing the autoharp," she was saying when everybody started laughing. Maybelle was flipping off the press without realizing it! She laughed as hard as anybody.

Music, of course, was a big part of Maybelle's life. She'd play her autoharp and even taught me to pick out a song or two. She played her guitar quite a bit, "to keep my fingers limber," she said.

Her favorite songs were "Single Girl, Married Girl," "Keep on the Sunnyside," "Wildwood Flower," and "Foggy Mountain Top." But the prettiest song I ever heard her play was "Bells of St. Mary's."

We listened to a lot of other people's music, at home and in the car. She liked the old-time Opry stars like Roy Acuff and Ernest Tubb and younger acts like the Statler Brothers and the Oak Ridge Boys. She loved Elvis.

As famous as she was, you couldn't tell by looking at her. It seems like it just never did dawn on her that she was famous. She never showed it, never talked about it, never, ever acted like it. She was really pretty quiet, even kind of shy. Despite her success, she stayed humble about what she'd accomplished.

She never talked about money, and wasn't extravagant

at all. She bought nice clothes (mostly black) but shopped at department stores like Harvey's and Cain-Sloan in Nashville or Norman's, a little dress shop in Madison.

Maybelle wasn't afraid of hard work. And she loved to clean. Mr. Carter didn't. Maybelle once told me he managed pretty good when she was on tour, but when she got home, the house looked like a tornado had hit it. She'd get it good and clean before the next tour.

Down in Jamaica, there was a man who lived in a cas-

I helped Maybelle and Jan Howard clean the Carter Museum.

tle—except it didn't have a roof and the floors were dirt. Maybelle and I and Connie Dickens (who was married to Little Jimmy Dickens) would go over to the castle and give it a good cleaning. We'd do our best to dust everything, polish the furniture, and sweep the dirt floor.

Another time they were planning a party at the Carter Museum in Hiltons, Virginia. Maybelle wasn't happy about how the place looked. So she put together a group including me, June, Opry star Jan Howard, and Sara Carter's daughter Janette. We cleaned that place from top to bottom.

Doing for others was important to Maybelle. She helped all her brothers and sisters, and gave anybody money if they needed it. She loved celebrating birthdays, Easter, and Christmas by giving everyone money. In the later years, June provided the money for her mom to give out.

Maybelle loved the valley where she grew up. We'd go back there every chance we got and stay at her sister's house for two or three weeks at a time, visiting kin and playing cards.

June's cousin Fern was married to Walt Salyers, one of my favorites. He was a big Johnny Cash fan, and he'd blast out his music so loud, you could hear it all over the valley.

The valley was really a beautiful place, especially in the fall when the leaves turned. There wasn't much flat land: The houses stood along the road, and the mountains rose up right behind them. One time Walt took me for a ride on his tractor all over the valley. I'll never forget what he said. "This is life. This is the way to live in this valley."

Maybelle's family came to Nashville to visit whenever they could. Her old singing partner and first cousin Sara Carter and Sara's husband Coy Bays came from California every year to see Maybelle and park their Airstream trailer in her backyard. Sara and Coy took their meals inside but slept in the trailer.

After each visit, Sara would ask me to bake two skillets of cornbread to last them all the way home.

Sara's last visit was early in 1978. She left with tears streaming down her face. "We'll never see each other alive again," she told Maybelle. She was right. Maybelle died in October and Sara died the next January.

The last few years of her life, Maybelle had Shy-Drager Syndrome, a degenerative disease of the brain. Her bladder was affected, and I used a catheter to empty it five times a day. We had to do it religiously or there would be trouble. In fact, one time down at New Port Richey we'd gone out to play bingo. While we were out a high tide came in and we couldn't get to the house. I had to get the police to ferry me to the house in a boat so I could get Maybelle's supplies.

Anyway, one day in October 1978 I was worried because there wasn't much urine. I called the doctor and he told me to give Maybelle a fluid pill. She wouldn't take it, though.

"I'll be up all night if I take that," she said. "Give it to me tomorrow."

I was making some pear preserves that day. You have to cook the pears in a real thick pot and watch them carefully or they'll scorch. About four-thirty Maybelle told me, "Peggy, you need to get me ready to go to bingo." I asked her if she was up to it. She said, "I'll be fine." I was getting her dressed when I smelled my pears scorching. They stuck a little, but Maybelle thought they'd be okay.

We went on to the VFW club and Maybelle won fifty dollars that night.

When we got back I made her one of her favorites, a steak sandwich with ketchup, and put her to bed. By that time we were sharing a king-size bed downstairs because she couldn't climb to the second floor anymore. She told me, as she did every night, "Goodnight, honey. I love you." Maybelle went to sleep happy.

I put my preserves in the jars and then went to bed beside her.

We both usually woke up about nine in the morning, but I didn't open my eyes until ten. "Something's wrong," I thought. Maybelle wouldn't wake up. I touched her hand, and it was cold. Her lips were blue and her face all swollen.

I was so scared I couldn't remember the number for 911. I called Minnie Snow and she came over with her gardener. By the time she got there, I had managed to call the paramedics and they were trying to revive Maybelle. But there was nothing they could do. She had died in her sleep there beside me. June told me later, "Only the godly go like that."

I never could eat those preserves.

* * *

That was a very hard time for me. Maybelle and I had been together day and night for nearly four years. Losing her was like losing my Mama. It about killed June too.

After the funeral we all went to John and June's home. They asked me to stay in the Due West house with Toob and Babe, and help out in the office. I took a few days off and then went to work in the museum and gift shop at the House of Cash.

Not long after Maybelle's death, John and June took me to Israel with them, a trip they made pretty often.

The trip came at a good time for me. I worked hard, stayed busy, and enjoyed my memories of Maybelle, the Mother of Country Music, who treated me like one of her daughters.

The Carter family tree

Alvin Pleasant Delaney Carter (1881–1960)
    Married Sara Elizabeth Dougherty (1898–1979) in 1915
        Gladys Carter born 1919
        Janette Carter born 1923
        Joe Carter born 1927

Ezra J. Carter (1896–1975)
    Married Maybelle Addington (1909–1978) in 1926
        Helen Carter born 1927, died 1998
        Valerie June Carter born 1929, died 2003
        Anita Carter born 1933, died 1999

The Carter Family

Maybelle Addington and her cousin Sara Dougherty were married to brothers Ezra and Alvin Pleasant Carter. Maybelle had taught herself to play guitar, creating a unique picking-and-strumming technique. She got together with Sara, who played autoharp and had a powerful alto voice, and A.P., who played fiddle and sang bass.

They played locally in Virginia until 1927, when the three of them traveled to Bristol, Tennessee, to audition for Ralph Peer of Victor Records. He recorded a handful of their songs.

The records sold pretty well, and A.P. talked Sara and Maybelle into going on the road. The Carter Family's career took off. But as it reached its peak in the late Thirties, Sara and A.P. got divorced. She still sang with The Carter Family until she retired in 1943.

Sara moved to California with her second husband Coy Bays, one of A.P.'s cousins. A.P. went back to Hiltons, Virginia, and ran a general store, which later became the Carter Family Museum. And Maybelle hit the road with daughters Helen, June, and Anita, performing as Mother Maybelle and the Carter Sisters.

Three Sisters

HELEN, JUNE, AND Anita Carter grew up on the road. In fact, Helen cut her first record before she was even born: Maybelle was pregnant with her when she, A.P. Carter, and her cousin Sara Carter made their first record in 1927.

When Maybelle, Sara, and A.P. went on the road as The Carter Family, Maybelle brought the girls with her. Many times after the show, Maybelle would go to put her guitar away and find Anita or June curled up in her guitar case sound asleep.

The girls started performing when they were just toddlers. By the time Anita and June were four or five years old, they were singing on the radio. All three of the girls were very talented. Helen played accordion and guitar. She played the most like Maybelle, using the "Carter scratch" that her mom invented. June played autoharp, banjo, guitar, piano, and harmonica. Anita played stand-up bass. I think she had the prettiest singing voice.

When she and the girls were touring as Mother Maybelle and the Carter Sisters, she drove them all over the country in her black Cadillac, she told me. There'd be herself and the three girls—and sometimes Chet Atkins when he played with them—all crammed in the car, with Anita's big bass fiddle sticking out the window.

They'd drive all night, stopping at truckstops along the way. No matter what time it was, they'd always meet some fans.

June takes the lead at a Carter Sisters concert.

Maybelle and the Carter Sisters in 1967

The three girls were a lot like their mama, always kind and thoughtful. I never heard them have much of a cross word with each other or raise their voices–except in song.

A couple of times on the road, though, Helen and her sister Anita got into it a little. At every show there'd be a bouquet of roses on the piano. I was rooming with Anita, and after the show she said, "Peggy, go get those roses for me. I want to look at them here in the room."

A few minutes after I got back, Helen called and said it wasn't fair for Anita to have all the flowers. "Anita, you're just a big baby and you always get whatever you want," she said. "I want some of those roses."

Anita gave in and I took about half of the roses down to Helen. I stuck them in a trash can, because that's the

Young June Carter meets young Dennis Devine for the first time.

only thing we had to carry them in. Helen looked them over and said, "That's not half of them." She was starting to pout.

I went back and reported this to Anita. "Fine," she snapped. "Just give her all of them then." I carried the rest of the roses down to Helen.

When I got back, Anita had been studying about it. "I don't think Helen needs all those roses. I want some of them back."

Back to Helen's room I went. Well, in the meantime she had cut the stems off so they would stand up in an ice bucket. I took exactly half of them back to Anita.

She took one look and said, "She's ruined them! I don't want them now; take them back to Helen."

I just smiled and dragged those roses back down the hall. You don't ever want to get caught between two sisters.

Another time I was driving the two of them around Los Angeles, Helen up front and her sister in the back. Anita, who had bad asthma, said she couldn't breathe. I turned the air conditioning up real high for her.

That started Helen off. "I'm freezing to death," she said and asked me to turn the air down.

"You want to kill me," Anita said.

I had to pull off the freeway onto the shoulder to get Anita's asthma medicine out of the trunk so they'd shut up.

June told me later Helen and Anita acted like that when they were little, too.

When we were touring I often drove for Helen and Anita. One time we were somewhere in New York trying to get to the next show, about a hundred fifty miles away. Anita was asleep in the back seat and Helen was navigating.

Well, we drove and we drove and we drove until finally Helen woke Anita up and told her she had to help us. We stopped at a little German restaurant to eat and try to find out where we were and how to get to where we were going.

We'd driven two hundred and fifty miles out of our

Helen Carter

Anita Carter

way. Helen blamed Anita. "We wouldn't have gotten lost if you'd been awake," she said.

"We might have gone two hundred fifty miles out of our way," Anita said, "but I sure enjoyed that sauerkraut."

The girls would tease each other about cleaning. June must have gotten her mom's cleaning gene: Maybelle laughed that as a kid June walked around all day with a broom in her hand. "Yeah," Helen would say, "but she'd sweep the dirt under a rug instead of in the dustpan." And June would point out that Anita always got out of a lot of housework. "That's because she's the baby," Maybelle would say. They laughed about that all the time.

Helen lived out of town, so we never saw her much except on tour. I got to know Anita pretty well, though.

Sometime around 1984, Toob and Babe went back to Virginia, and June gave the house where we three had been living to her daughter Carlene. This was the house June bought when she was married to Carlene's daddy, Carl Smith.

I was looking for a place to live when Anita asked me to stay with her. Her son Jay is autistic, and I could help her out with him when I wasn't on the road with John and June.

I still talk to Jay several times a week and take him out to dinner just about every week. He's super-smart in some ways, and reads the *Guinness World Records* cover to cover every year. He's very good with details, and is always trying to talk me into going to Las Vegas with him so we can win a fortune like Rainman in the Dustin Hoffman movie.

He writes me letters in the most precise handwriting you've ever seen (especially near his birthday when he sends a list), but if he makes a single mistake he has to start over. He has sent me an elaborate drawing of a bowling alley, complete to the tiny clips holding potato chip bags on the counter.

Sometimes his enthusiasm gets him in a little trouble. He loves cars and is always telling me to get a Cadillac. One day I got a call from a car dealer saying my car was ready. Jay had ordered me a Cadillac with all the extras!

One thing that Helen and Anita always agreed on: Daddy's little girl—the one Mr. Carter was partial to ever since she was young—was their middle sister, Valerie June.

Sweet June Blue-Eyes

JUNE WAS MOTHER to us all. The kids, the family, friends, staff, fans, people she just saw on the street—everybody came under her wing.

June couldn't stand for anybody to hurt or be in need. She was always there with money, or a prayer, or a helping hand, or a kind word.

One example was Connie Dickens, who'd been friends with June for fifty years. After she was divorced from Little Jimmy Dickens, Connie went out to Texas and started running around drinking.

"I don't want Connie out there by herself," June said. She sent somebody down to Texas to bring her back to Hendersonville. She set Connie up in a house and gave her a job at the Amqui Station Antique Store.

June never said no to anybody who needed help. And no matter how much somebody let her down, June would still be there for them.

I think part of it goes back to her roots: a small moun-

tain community where everybody knew their neighbors and everybody took care of each other.

She had good raising, too. Maybelle was one of the kindest people I ever met, and June was just like her.

June's hobbies were flowers and shopping. She was very good at both.

She loved fresh flowers, and put them in every room of the house. When we were home in Hendersonville, we'd go down to Smith and Rogers every week and buy two or three hundred dollars' worth of cut flowers, especially daisies and chrysanthemums. They'd fill the whole back seat and trunk of the Mercedes.

I'd ask her, "June, what are we going to do with all these flowers?" She'd always say, "Honey, we'll find a home for them."

And she did. She had a real gift for arranging flowers. They'd end up looking like a florist did them. She collected vases of every size, and she'd carefully match bouquets to vases. She put arrangements in every room of the house: bedrooms, dining rooms, kitchen, den, bathrooms. For her bathroom she'd put them in small vases and line the edges of the bathtub.

As soon as they started wilting, we'd go get some more.

Outside, she had baskets of ferns and flowers hanging everywhere and planted pansies and petunias all over. She had a knack for knowing just where to plant something to make it look good.

Her favorite flowers were tube roses. When they were in bloom she filled the house with them. They gave the whole house a wonderful smell, especially at night. She kept us busy planting them in the summer, then digging them up every fall to dry and save.

In Jamaica, all kinds of flowers grew wild, so we just cut them from the yard. June took bushes and tree branches and made beautiful bouquets.

Her other passion was shopping. Everywhere we went, she'd go shopping first thing. She really had a lot of stuff. She loved stuff, and she loved to give people their own stuff.

She'd buy a lot of linens at Old Time Pottery in Madison, mostly so she'd have gifts for other people. And any

June surrounded herself with crystal, china, and fine furniture.

time she took somebody shopping with her, she'd urge them to pick something out and let her buy it for them.

She collected pretty things: fine linens, many sets of sterling and crystal, dozens of sterling silver serving pieces. She probably had two hundred sets of fine china.

They weren't just for looking at, either. She insisted we use them every day. We'd set the dinner table with linen cloths and napkins, sterling silver, fine china, and crystal, whether we were in Hendersonville, Florida, or Jamaica.

Even when we ate on trays—which didn't happen very often—we'd have linen placemats under the fine china.

When my sister Betty first started working for June, we all went up to the Mountain House to give it a thorough cleaning. June decided to have a luncheon to welcome Betty, so she sent us back to Hendersonville with a list: tablecloth, real china, sterling silverware, and stem glasses. The only problem was, we didn't have a big enough table in the Mountain House.

June found a great big stump out in the yard. She draped it with a linen tablecloth and put out her place settings. We certainly ate in style, out in the yard on a stump.

She bought most of her clothes ready-made, mainly in New York or California. She had a knack for picking out clothes that she'd look good in, so she always looked pretty. She could even put on clothes that nobody else looked good in, fix them up with a pretty scarf, and look like a million bucks.

She collected furs, and John loved to buy them for her.

John loved to add to June's fur collection.

Every so often, she'd buy up a bunch of furs in New York and throw a fur party in Hendersonville. She'd invite two or three hundred people—mostly close friends and entertainers' wives—to a fur show and sale. We'd make a sit-down lunch for all of them, usually beef tenderloin, green beans, homemade rolls, and a dessert.

Other times she'd have linen, crystal, or jewelry parties. A couple of times a year we'd have a luncheon and sale.

She'd also have antique parties and invite friends to see them and buy them. She'd display the antiques on one dining table and serve an elegant meal on another table.

June loved antiques. She spent a lot of time—and

June reads from her book *From the Heart*. She could make any outfit look good.

money–hunting for antique silver, china, crystal, and especially beds. She had a real thing about pretty beds, and she bought solid-wood poster beds that she could "pretty up," as she called it. Almost every bedroom in every house they owned had two double beds, and one had three.

"At one particular time, I had a hundred and twenty beds," she told me once.

Most of the beds had canopies she made herself. And each one had an antique spread or quilt she'd collected. She changed them around right often, but then June was always changing something.

Her antique collection got so huge they had to find a place for it. The railroad had given John an old train station from the city of Amqui, just outside Madison. He had it moved lock, stock, and barrel to the grounds of the House of Cash, and they turned it into an antique store.

June also loved giving parties. It made her happy to see everybody get together and talk, enjoy good food, and have a good time. Sometimes I think she just wanted to have people around her.

It wasn't unusual to have seated dinners for two hundred fifty people. We'd cover the pool tables with fine linens and make them buffet tables. The silver was always wrapped in linen napkins and placed on sterling silver trays.

For bigger parties, weddings, and receptions, we went outside. We'd get a tent to cover the tennis courts overlooking the lake. These events were usually catered.

She loved playing hostess—putting everything in order, getting ready before the guests got there, and making sure everything went right. Everybody always had fun at June's

John's mother, at left in the blue dress, and Rodney Crowell, center, are among guests enjoying one of June's tent parties.

parties—without a drop of liquor! That's right. All they ever served was sparkling apple cider, iced tea, and soft drinks.

Not many people know how creative June was. She could take almost anything and make it look really pretty. She loved to create things from linen tablecloths she bought in Jamaica: lampshades, drapes, canopies for beds. She especially liked white linen tablecloths, and she'd buy several and sew them together to fit her big tables. She'd give them to her friends as Christmas presents and use them herself.

She made all the curtains and some of the bedspreads in the Jamaica house. The master bedroom in Henderson-ville had twelve huge plate-glass windows that June made drapes for. It took twenty-four tablecloths; she used matching napkins for the tie-backs.

Jamaica also supplied the materials for a beautiful coffee table June made. We were down there when they bulldozed the site for a new golf course. The dozers turned up garbage dumps from the elegant houses of the seventeenth and eighteenth centuries, and I'd go over there and poke through the dirt for pieces of glass and china.

The Jamaica house had a real long coffee table with a glass top. I took the top off it for June and got some putty at the hardware store. I'd carry the table out on the porch, and June worked on it out there. She created beautiful designs from the pieces of china. I bet that table weighed a hundred pounds when she was done with it.

June's favorite song was Maybelle's "Wildwood Flower." And she really liked her sister Anita's version of Maybelle's "I'll Be All Smiles Tonight." (Maybelle once told me that many songs written by her and Sara were credited to A.P. Carter because women couldn't sign contracts in those days.)

She'd listen to some of John's music, and George Jones and Kris Kristofferson.

June loved being on stage. She really lit up in front of an audience. But she hated to hear herself sing. "I can't hardly stand to hear myself sing," she'd say. "I sound terrible."

I think June felt she wasn't as good a singer as her

mama and sisters, and that's why she started a comedy routine as a teenager. She had a natural gift for it. She played

Audiences—and John—loved June's Aunt Polly character.

Aunt Polly Carter, a hillbilly lady wearing crazy clothes. When she started touring with John, he asked her to revive the routine, which was always a big hit with the audience.

June loved to dance around the house. Sometimes she'd put on a tape and just start dancing. Before we knew it, everybody in the kitchen had joined in. John just laughed at us, and sometimes he'd dance a little too.

June was always acting silly around the house, and she could go into a fit of giggles over the least little thing, usually something she'd just said or done.

Although she laughed and carried on a lot, June's spirits got down sometimes. If John was sick, she got down. When one of the kids was in trouble, she got down.

June almost never lost her cool. If she did, it was usually over one of the children. She'd tell me, "That made me angry." Saying this was about as mad as she ever got. No tears, no yelling, just "That made me angry." Then she'd let it roll off her and she'd be fine.

She got really depressed after Helen and Anita died. "I can't believe my sisters are gone," she'd say several times a day. "Now I'm the only one left." She would play the old Carter recordings, and that seemed to cheer her up.

June loved the mountains as much as her mama and daddy did. Virginia meant home to her, and it meant family.

For many years we'd return to the home place in Poor Valley to celebrate June's birthday. John knew how happy going back to Hiltons, Virginia, made June, especially after her sisters died and she was feeling all alone.

John's daughter Kathy would bring her family, and John Carter and his family would come up. June's cousin Esther would always come in.

All the cousins and other kin would get together for a covered dish luncheon. They'd put up a tent and borrow tables and chairs from the funeral home. Most of the people in the Valley came, with pans of fried chicken and fresh cooked vegetables from their gardens. Cousin Mary always brought her coconut cream pie.

John loved June's kinfolks, particularly Joe Carter, A.P.'s son.

Whenever we were in Poor Valley, it didn't matter what time we got up, Joe Carter would be sitting on the porch by the back door. Betty and I would sit and drink coffee with him until John got up and joined us.

After he'd had some coffee John would ask, "Joe, would you like some country ham, biscuits, and gravy? Peggy will make us up some."

We returned to the valley where June grew up for her birthdays.

Well, Joe always stopped for breakfast at a little restaurant down the road before he came by. That didn't stop
him, though; he'd eat again with us.

If they weren't doing anything else, John and Joe
would get out the Jeep and go mountain climbing. Or
they'd drive all around the Holston River.

Sometimes John would say, "Let's go float." We'd get
the kinfolk and kids together three to a fishing boat and
float down the Holston. The water was so clear you could
see the fish swimming from the boat.

Joe would come back at night and have supper with
us. Then he and John would sit outside singing, talking
about music, and writing songs.

When they could, John and June would perform at

June joins A.P. Carter's children Janette and Joe on stage at the
Carter Fold as John watches from off stage.

the Carter Fold. John said he always liked going to the Fold because it was such a clean place with no drinking or fighting. Joe's sister Janette kept an eye on people, and was known to talk people right off the floor if she thought they were dancing too close together.

Joe and Janette would sing and Joe would do his comedy routine. He was real good at making sounds with his mouth.

He had this big old handlebar mustache, and he'd pull on it and shake it while imitating a dog and cat fighting. He also made sounds like a pig. He'd finish the act by mimicking a coffeepot perking, then bring June and John on stage.

John always got so tickled. "I just love hearing old Joe do that," he'd say.

We'd see Tom T. Hall and his wife Dixie while we were up there. They have a place in Hiltons, and Tom T. comes over to the Carter Fold every morning after a show to help clean up. Dixie always fixes food for the Carter Family Festival held the first weekend in August.

We always had a good time when we went up there, and it was good for June.

June was always so kind, and good to everybody. She was a good woman. And it's a cliché but it's true what they say: Behind every good man is a good woman. John R. Cash was a good man, and she always stood behind him.

The Man in Black

THE WORLD KNEW him as Johnny Cash, but he was always John to me.

He was a good guy, easy to get along with, and always nice to people. He was a great boss, not too demanding, and was good to all his employees, including me.

Next to June, family and friends were the most important things in John's life. He gathered them around him, and he took care of them all he could.

He gave jobs to every member of his family who wanted one, and he still supported them even after they left. He kept Maybelle, Helen, and Anita on the payroll until the day they died, long after they stopped singing with him.

I was always touched by his thoughtfulness. I had my tonsils out, believe it or not, when I was fifty-three years old. Before I went to the hospital, John told me, "Peggy, I can't be there for the surgery, but I'll be there when you wake up."

John and the Tennessee Three, Luther Perkins, W.D. Holland, and Marshall Grant, signed fan Dennis Devine's concert program.

Sure enough, I opened my eyes in the recovery room and John was sitting there holding my hand.

Then he laughed and asked me if I wanted some popcorn.

He even took time to visit my mama in the nursing home, and helped her celebrate her eightieth birthday in Baptist Hospital.

John liked to call the shots, and he could be difficult if he didn't get his way. He thought he should do what he wanted to do instead of what other people wanted or expected him to do.

When he got upset, he'd be grumpy with everybody,

giving short answers or none at all. But he got over it pretty fast, and then he'd come around saying he was sorry for the way he'd been acting.

He was never really gifted about doing work.

He was a real hard worker on stage, but when it came to putting gas in the car or something like that, he wasn't much interested. But, as June said more than once, "he always provided for us."

He wasn't real handy around the house. I never knew him to mow the yard or use the weedeater. But when we had new pictures to hang, John always wanted to be the one to put them up. He didn't know a thing about nails, and he'd pick one big enough to build a house with. The

June and John help my mother celebrate her eightieth birthday.

pictures ended up kind of helter-skelter but John was happy.

He mostly stayed out of the kitchen. He'd roast himself some peanuts or make some popcorn, but that was about it. He helped make homemade ice cream by watching the electric freezer.

He'd try to make coffee, with mixed results. Sometimes he'd put the grounds where the water went and pour the water in on top. One time, the pot got stopped up, and you've never seen such a mess. Coffee grounds were everywhere: the counter, the front of the cabinet, all over the floor.

John reunited with his Sun labelmates Carl Perkins, left, and Jerry Lee Lewis, far right.

"What in the world happened?" I asked him. He acted surprised. "Did I do that?" he said. "I should have known better."

The only dish he ever made was his famous chili. He went heavy on the peppers and chili powder–he liked it so hot that June couldn't eat it. It was a big production, too. He'd crush each of the tomatoes with his hands, squirting stuff everywhere. When he got to the last tomato, he'd give it a big kiss before he threw it in the pot.

He didn't do much grocery shopping by himself, but he'd run down the street from our house in Hendersonville to a little fruit stand run by the Mennonites. He bought mostly honey, jelly, and peanuts. He always bought a watermelon or two–he really loved their melons.

Every now and then he'd drive to Center Point Barbecue in Hendersonville. One time he asked them if they'd make him some pork rinds the next time they cooked shoulders. After that, they'd trim the skin off, cut it into strips, and fry them up for him, then give him a call every time a new batch was ready.

John had to change his diet when he was diagnosed with diabetes. He was pretty good about cutting out sugar, but I had to watch him when he went grocery shopping with me because he'd sneak candy into the basket. He just loved circus peanuts, those big orange puffy things.

"John, you know you can't eat those with your diabetes," I'd tell him.

"Oh, I'll just eat one or two," he'd promise me. Then he'd eat a whole bag on the way home.

Other times he'd buy a big pack of Juicy Fruit and chew every piece until the sugar was gone and spit the gum out the car window. He'd go through a whole pack before we got back home.

He kept his diabetes under control pretty well, but around 2001 it started affecting his eyes. John came in one day and said, "Y'all are going to have to start driving. I saw double while I was driving today and I don't want to drive anymore.

"I'm afraid I'll hurt somebody," he said.

He really didn't like having to rely on someone else to get around. "I hate it that I can't drive, but it's better for my safety and everybody else's," he told me.

John never acted like he had a lot of money. He wasn't real showy about money. Jay Davis, Anita's autistic son, once asked him, "Johnny Cash, are you rich? Do you have two million dollars?"

John said, "Yes, son, I do have money."

He liked telling this story. "Jay's the only person who ever asked me that," he told me.

John was always free with his money—sometimes too free. When he pulled his clothes off at night, he'd just drop them where he stood, not emptying out the pockets or anything. He always carried a Swiss Army Knife, and we must have washed it a hundred times.

Well, one day my sister Shirley picked up his clothes and washed them, and when she opened the dryer, hundred dollar bills started flying everywhere. John had left two thousand dollars in his pocket; the twenty bills were now nice and clean.

Other than that, he was pretty neat around the house. He was good about putting towels and dirty clothes in the basket. He also kept his closet straight, not much clutter.

He'd always ask for help packing his clothes for a tour, but when I'd get up to his room he'd be mostly done. He'd have his pants and shirts packed in the suitcase, as neat as when Shirley hung them up.

Speaking of clothes, a fan once said, "Johnny Cash,

A lucky Grand Ole Opry audience saw June, Helen, and Anita sing backup for Waylon Jennings, center, John, and Roy Acuff.

since you're the Man in Black I guess you wear black underwear too." John laughed and said, "No, I don't wear any underwear at all." People thought he was kidding, but I know it's true, because I never washed or packed a single pair of underwear for him.

John loved to collect things. He liked silver dollars and gold bricks. He also collected knives and guns. He kept those at the House of Cash. He'd pull them out to look at, but he didn't shoot much at all.

He enjoyed antiquing with June. They bought a ton of antiques when we were on tour overseas, especially in England and Belgium. He collected sideboards, and a lot of them. He and June would fill up all the houses and line the walls at the Museum, and put the rest of them in the antique store.

John was a great big man: six foot three and two-twenty or two hundred thirty pounds. He was big-boned, with a big frame, but he had skinny little chicken legs.

On stage he always had that big, booming voice. He'd say, "Hello, I'm Johnny Cash," in what many described as the voice of God. But you know, at home he actually had a soft, almost gentle voice.

He'd call for me sometimes using his Johnny Cash voice. He'd holler "HELLO! Anybody home?" I'd come see what he wanted, and he'd laugh and say, "Nothing, I just wanted to see if you'd run away."

He had a great sense of humor.

He laughed at June's corny jokes–the only kind she knew. And her Aunt Polly routines just cracked him up.

He could be a little bawdy. He'd spell a naughty word playing Scrabble just for a joke. Sometimes he'd tell me and Betty a dirty joke. June would be scandalized. "John, where did you get that?" she'd say. "I can't believe you're telling them jokes with those bad words in them!" He'd just laugh.

John was incredibly forgiving. He was having some dental work done one time and the dentist broke his jaw. It gave John quite a bit of pain in the later years–the side of his face looks swollen and angry in pictures from that time. But he never held it against the dentist. "That's just one of those things," John said. He and June both continued to see him as long as they lived, flying up to New York two or three times a year.

John had surgery a couple of times to try to repair the damage. Before the operation, the surgeon was explaining that he would take bone from John's hip and put it in his jaw. John said, "If you take bone from my hip, my jaw will always be wanting to sit down."

His jaw was just one of his many health problems, and doctors were always prescribing pain killers. With his history, it was easy for John to get addicted again. But he and June knew the warning signs. Two or three times while I was with him, he'd say, "I have to get off this pain medicine." He'd check into the Betty Ford Center for a few weeks to shake the addiction.

Once he was there at the same time as Elizabeth Tay-

John's once-broken jaw gave him a lot of pain in later years, but he kept smiling.

lor. They were assigned to trash detail together. That must have been a sight: the famous Johnny Cash and the legendary Elizabeth Taylor, taking out the garbage.

Except for his two or three relapses, in more than

thirty years I never saw John on hard drugs. Outsiders "knew" all about his drug problem, but the truth is, he'd been mostly clean since the Seventies.

More than once he said, "It was with the help of June, Maybelle, Mr. Carter, and God that I got off drugs."

He never talked much about those early days. But one day in Jamaica we were talking about things young people did, and he told me, "I can't say too much, 'cause when I was using I did a lot of wild things myself."

He went on to say, "I don't know why I ever used pills." He blamed the music business, since you have to be on the go all the time. "You've got to travel, you've got to find time to sleep, and you've got to be ready to go when it's time to take the stage," he said.

John didn't have music playing all the time. I think sometimes he just wanted to take a break from his job. That's how John always looked at making music. "I'm just earning a living," he'd say.

Emmylou Harris was John's favorite singer, and he loved anything that Sheryl Crow did. He listened a lot to black gospel groups, plus country and bluegrass. Really, he'd listen to almost anything except classical. He liked what he called "plain old songs."

He played newer groups like the Statler Brothers and the Oak Ridge Boys and the old-timers like Hoyt Axton, Roy Acuff, and Ernest Tubb.

I'd hear John singing in the shower all the time. He'd usually sing his songs or Carter family favorites.

One of his songs he would *not* sing was "Dirty Old Egg-Sucking Dog." He absolutely hated it. He told me, "I don't know why I ever recorded that song."

John was always writing songs. He'd sit out on the porch in Jamaica or by the lake in Hendersonville and sing to himself, then write it down. He kept a pad by the bed because he'd wake up in the night thinking about a song and get up to write the words down.

He recorded his songs all over the place. The House of Cash had a studio set up, and John had equipment at the Hendersonville house, the Mountain House, the Compound, and Mrs. Cash's house. Late in his life, I rode him in a golf cart to Marty Stuart's house next door for a session.

One of his favorite studios was at Jack "Cowboy" Clements in Nashville. Cowboy called me up one time and asked me if I would make a pot of pinto beans and some cornbread and bring them with John to a session.

John was real business-like in the studio; he didn't do much clowning around. He was real good about getting songs down in one or two takes.

Most people didn't know it, but John was really very shy. That made him kind of quiet. I've known him to sit in a house full of people and go for hours without saying a word.

He didn't mind being by himself; in fact, he liked it. He'd go down to the Bon Aqua farm or the Mountain House for days at a time. He'd read and write, and sometimes just sit on the porch listening to the crickets and frogs. He always said it was so peaceful there.

That's probably why he liked fishing so much—there's not a lot of talking involved.

John's Family

JOHN REALLY LOVED his family and tried hard to take care of them. He'd visit his parents every day at their house down the road.

John's mom Carrie Cash was a big, strong woman. She'd slap you on the back and nearly knock you down. If she hugged you, she'd about break your back.

She was stern—when she said something, you knew she meant it. And yet she was also very kind.

People would say to her, "You must be very proud of Johnny." She'd always say, "I'm proud of all six of my children." But I knew that John was her favorite: She was always partial to J.R., as she called him.

That's actually the name on his birth certificate. The story goes that she and her husband couldn't agree on a name and finally just said "J.R." As a youngster he became known as "John" and was renamed "Johnny" by producer Sam Phillips of Sun Studio. The "R" never stood for anything as far as I know.

Mrs. Cash's slap on the back would knock you down, but she was very kind.

John credited his mama with inspiring his interest in music. I can still see her sitting tall on her piano bench pounding the keys as John stood beside her singing the old songs from his childhood.

Mrs. Cash loved to work in the gift shop at the House of Cash. She was very competitive about it; she wanted her cash register total to be higher than anyone else's. She complained in the evening if it wasn't. I think she just loved making all that money for John.

Finally, John had to pull me aside and tell me, "Peggy, I hate to hit you with this, but is there any way you could let Mama have more sales?" My sister Betty and I already were just selling admission tickets to the museum, and we couldn't help but sell a lot of tickets. It was hard to let her come out on top. So Betty and I would go extra slow, and send people over to her register to get rung up whenever we could.

Anyway, Mrs. Cash went to H.G. Hill grocery store nearly every day. She liked to have fresh fruit, so she'd buy just two of whatever she was getting, two bananas, two pears, two apples—one for her and one for her husband.

One day, she was on her way back from the store and saw that a tour bus had pulled up in front of the House of Cash. She knew that meant a lot of sales. She screeched into the parking lot, jumped out, and ran inside to her register.

The next day she came to me with a funny little smile. "Well, I didn't have to start my car last night," she told me. She'd been so excited when she pulled in the parking lot that she forgot to turn the motor off. The car ran for hours and was still going strong at the end of the day.

We sold souvenir cards five for a dollar in the gift shop. A woman really wanted the cards, but her husband wouldn't let her spend a dollar. Mrs. Cash was disgusted. "I'd take my walking stick to him if that was my husband," she said.

Her husband Ray was a real gentle man. Mrs. Cash was quite a bit taller than he was, and I'm sure she made him walk the line.

I think he was probably a little rough on his kids

Mr. Cash was a cool little man. Behind him you can see the cotton he always planted at the House of Cash.

growing up. They learned to work hard: John once told me about picking cotton as a kid to help make ends meet.

He and his dad remembered their roots. The House of Cash had a horseshoe driveway, and every year Mr. Cash would bring cotton seeds from his Arkansas farm and plant them inside the horseshoe. After his dad died in 1985, John planted the cotton himself every year. There was a big old bowl outside the Jamaica house, and John always planted cotton seed there in memory of his dad.

Mr. Cash was a cool little man. He sat out on his porch every day and waved at the tour buses going by his and John's houses. There must be an awful lot of pictures of him in this world because fans would be hanging out the windows with their cameras.

He chewed tobacco while he was out there, spitting his chaw over the rose bush at the end of the porch. He always sized you up by whether you could spit over the bush. I went by their house sometimes to chew with him, and showed him I could spit.

Mr. Cash had Parkinson's Disease and finally had to go to a nursing home. John and I went to visit him one day and he was dying for a chew of tobacco he had stashed. I rounded up some styrofoam cups, and the three of us sat around chewing for a while.

Mrs. Cash dipped snuff but she didn't want people to know it. But one day I saw her little snuff box and the secret was out.

They were quite a pair. Every morning they'd get up at four o'clock. Breakfast was always oatmeal or cereal. If I dropped by to check on them in the morning, they'd offer me breakfast and make me a piece of toast.

I stayed with Mr. and Mrs. Cash one time when they were under the weather. Mr. Cash had a foot allergy, and I'd soak his feet in a tub and then rub lotion on them. Mrs. Cash got jealous of all the attention he was getting, so she made me rub her feet, too!

They both loved iced tea, but not the same iced tea, so they kept two pitchers in the refrigerator, his and hers, weak and strong. And they both wanted you to drink *their* iced tea. "Have you had some of my tea yet?" one would ask. "Have you tried some of mine?" said the other. I got to where I mixed the two teas together to satisfy them.

* * *

John's brother Roy worked at the House of Cash.

Roy's granddaughter Kellye Cash was Miss America.

The House of Cash was a real family affair. Nearly all of John's brothers and sisters and some of his in-laws worked there at one time or another.

His brother Roy was the manager of the museum for years and years. He was a real nice guy. Roy's grand-daughter, Kellye Cash, was Miss America in 1987. People wrote in after that saying John had bought her the title, but he didn't have a thing to do with it.

Louise was John's oldest sister. She looked just like her mother, tall and straight with white hair. Her husband Joe did maintenance at the House of Cash and worked on John's farm. One time he got off his tractor to open a gate. Just as he walked in front of the tractor, it jumped into gear and ran right over him. He broke about every bone in his body but he survived.

Reba and Joanne were John's little sisters. Reba managed the House of Cash for forty years or more, and her daughter Kelly worked as John's secretary for a while. Joanne worked there years ago, and she's involved now

John's sister Joanne helps me celebrate my birthday.

with the Nashville Cowboy Church she founded with her husband.

Tommy Cash was John's little brother. He never worked at the House of Cash: He had his own music career. But he was in and out all the time, and we saw a lot of him.

Whether they worked for him or not, John took care of his family. He always made sure they had what they needed.

The Cash family tree

Ray Cash (1897–1985)

Married Carrie Cloverlee Rivers (1904–1991) in 1920

Roy Cash born 1921, died 1993

Margaret Louise Cash born 1924, died 2003

Jack D. Cash born 1929, died 1944

J.R. Cash, born 1932, died 2003

Rebecca Ann (Reba) Cash, born 1934

Joanne Cash, born 1938

Tommy Cash, born 1940

Hand in Hand

JOHN AND JUNE'S life together meant more than anything else to them. You never saw one of them without the other, especially early in their marriage.

They went for long walks holding hands, exploring when they were on tour or just wandering around the Compound when they were at home.

They loved going places with each other–shopping, visiting Maybelle, getting John Carter at school, going to the grocery store.

They'd go to New York for two or three weeks or head for California on a vacation. They used to go to the Bon Aqua farm by themselves and stay for days at a time.

If someone told them about a new play or movie, they'd just jet up to New York to see it. They also went to the movies at home, in Hendersonville or nearby Rivergate. They'd settle in with a big Coke and a large popcorn. I think John went for the popcorn as much as anything: He loved it almost as much as roasted peanuts.

They didn't go out to eat much when they were at home, mostly because they ate out so much on the road. But they liked to go to Olive Garden, El Chico, and Outback Steakhouse. For a fancy evening they'd eat at Mario's, an exclusive Italian restaurant in Nashville.

They were really a romantic couple but not overly affectionate in public. She always called him "Honey" and he called her "Babe."

They loved candles, lit them in every room and all the way up the staircase. Sometimes there were so many it looked like a fortune-teller's tent.

Sadly, the last two or three years most of their dates were held in the hospital. Betty would bring John down to

John and June meet Prince Charles at a reception during a tour in New Brunswick, Canada.

see June for a while. By the time she got him back home he was ready to go see June again. So back they'd come.

They were always in love—to the very end.

Both John and June were really down to earth. At heart they were normal people, country people.

They always remembered their roots: "I was raised in a cotton patch and June was raised in Poor Valley," John would say. They never acted like they had a lot of money, never talked about what they had or how much.

But they didn't worry about spending it, either. June bought pretty much anything she wanted, and John never said a word more than "Go for it, Babe."

He loved buying stuff for June: clothes, jewelry, antiques, you name it. One time she said something about a sewing machine. He went straight to Jo-Ann Fabrics in Rivergate and bought the most expensive model for their anniversary.

Once in Europe June saw a string of pearls she really liked. John bought them for her on the spot, and didn't blink at the thirty thousand dollar price tag.

Their favorite hobby was spending money. It didn't matter where—they were just as happy buying clothes at Wal-Mart as shopping at the fanciest stores in New York.

They never put on like they were famous, never made a big show about who they were.

When we went to a restaurant, John would get embarrassed if the hostess recognized him and tried to seat him ahead of anybody else.

"We'll just wait our turn," he'd say.

They never acted like they were above people, but they never acted like they were much below people either. John met each of the last seven presidents, and he and June ran into Prince Charles one time in Canada, but they weren't particularly impressed. Their favorite president was Jimmy Carter. June once told him they were distant cousins, and he started calling her "Cousin" whenever they met.

They reflected each other a lot. If I paid attention to one of them, the other wanted it too. If June got upset, then John did too.

They were also like that about being sick. If June got a headache, ten minutes later John had a headache. One night June ate something and went to bed sick, saying she had food poisoning. John got up the next morning and said he'd caught the food poisoning from June.

They were the same way about the children. Whenever June did something for her kids, John had to do the same for his. They got pretty competitive about it, but they always ended up helping each other.

Though they didn't attend church much, John and June were religious people.

When he was a boy, John's family always went to church. John first got started singing in church; even when he was a teenager he had a real deep voice.

Mr. Cash once told me John read the whole Bible

John helps June with her boot on stage.

when he was young. He continued to read scripture all his life; I think he knew as much about the Bible as his good friend Billy Graham. John always watched Graham's Crusades when they were on television.

John was an ordained minister, and he took his duties

seriously. Whenever we visited Israel, he baptized people in the River Jordan.

They didn't go to church regularly, but John and June visited Jimmy Snow's Evangel Temple when they had a chance. If they went somewhere else, they didn't seek out any certain denomination: Baptist, Church of God, Assembly of God, and the Cowboy Church run by John's sister Joanne and her husband Harry Yates were some of the faiths they visited.

When we were on the road we'd find a church and go, or we'd have a prayer service at the hotel. At home, John and June would sometimes conduct a service in their house on Sunday mornings. John or June would give a devotion lesson, June would lead us in prayer, and we'd wind it up singing gospel songs.

Toward the end of his life, every time John said the blessing, he'd finish by asking God to help him with his ego! June and I would just look at each other and roll our eyes—we never understood where that was coming from.

June was a believer. We never sat down to a meal without blessing the food, whether we were on the road, out in the yard, or in the house.

When she was having trouble like one of the kids was acting up, or when someone she knew was in need, June turned to prayer. Sometimes she'd call her friends and family together to pray for someone they knew.

I never heard them argue. About the only time they got upset with each other was over how to handle the kids.

John and June smooch during a performance.

They wouldn't fight; they just wouldn't talk. Or I could tell by their tone of voice something had come between them. But that never lasted long.

They had their differences. June talked to anybody that would talk, but John wouldn't. When they ran into fans, June would stop and talk all day if she could.

John was actually kind of shy. He'd ask if they had something for him to sign and then head for the bus. After a while June would come report everything she'd learned.

He always said that June did the talking, and he did the listening. "I can get up on stage and sing and talk to a hundred thousand people," he once told me, "but it's so hard to sit down and talk to just one person."

June danced every night on stage, but John had two

left feet. He was stiff as a board on stage; all he could do was wiggle a little.

June hated smoking, especially in her house, but John was more tolerant. He used to be a heavy smoker and still liked to be around people who smoked. Some of the girls would go outside for a cigarette break. One day June came wandering through and asked, "Honey, where did everybody go?"

"Oh, those butt-suckers are outside," he said.

"John, that's not very nice."

"It's the truth," he said. "They're out there sucking on the butts of cigarettes, and I wish I could be out there smoking with them!"

My sister Betty was one of those butt-suckers. One time she and I were staying the night at the Hendersonville house because the weather was real bad. June had gone up to bed but John was still up. Betty headed outside to smoke.

"Betty, it's cold and snowing out there," he said. "You can smoke in the house." Well, she wouldn't do it because she knew June didn't want her to. He said she could stand by the fireplace.

A little later I came through the room and didn't see Betty. I hollered for her and heard her voice say "Over here." She had crawled into the big fireplace and was standing with her head up the chimney, blowing her smoke out. She assured me John had said it was okay for her to smoke in the house.

John was a real early riser; June would sleep in a lit-

The couple was inseparable for more than thirty years.

tle. Most mornings John would take her coffee up to her. He lost about half of it on the stairs, but June was always touched by his kindness.

They were both thoughtful like that. June started every day saying, "John, what can I do for you today?"

I think June and John felt guilty sometimes about taking over my life. John kept telling me he was going to find me a rich old man to marry. "What do you want in a man, Peggy?" he asked.

"A lot of hair, no false teeth, and plenty of money," I told him.

From time to time he'd come up with a name and ask me if I wanted him to fix me up. I finally told him, "John, I ain't looking for anybody and I want you to quit looking for me. I'm not ready to get married; I'm too young."

I did date a guy on and off for about eleven years but I got tired of waiting on him. He was faithful to his mother and his grandmother, and I knew he'd never marry anybody until something happened to them. And he didn't.

June worried about me, too. She felt me out one time when she was sitting with me in the hospital. "While I was waiting for you to wake up, I made up my mind to ask you if you ever wanted to get married," she told me later. "I knew that I'd get an honest answer while you were still waking up." I don't remember it, but she told me I said I didn't want to get married. I guess that made her feel better; she said, "Honey, that's good enough for me."

After knowing them for more than thirty years, I think what still impresses me the most was their incredible kindness, their willingness to help people out, and their generosity.

Generosity

JOHN AND JUNE were two of the most generous people I ever met. The wealthier they got, the more they used their riches to help others.

John was always glad he had the means to take care of people. And I think June just loved everybody, something she got from her mother.

Maybelle was kind to everyone, and she taught all her girls to be kind, too. In more than ten years together, I never heard Maybelle say anything bad about anybody. June was the same way. If I had my feelings hurt by somebody, she'd say, "Honey, just let it roll off your back like water off a duck."

June was always reaching out. One time when John Carter was eight or nine years old, June asked me to take her to pick him up at his school, Goodpasture Christian School in Madison.

We didn't get very far before we had a flat tire on Gallatin Pike. June flagged down a pickup truck for a ride.

The driver only had two teeth in his head. Well, he gave us a ride to the House of Cash just down the road, and when we got out June tried to pay him but he wouldn't take any money. She said to him, "Honey, thank you for the ride. If you ever need anything, you just come and ask me."

"Oh, June," I laughed as he drove off. "He'll probably come back and ask you for a whole new set of teeth."

She said, "Honey, if he does, I'll get him some new teeth."

Another time we were on tour in Germany. The bus passed a man on the side of the road. "That guy looks hungry," June said. "Don't you think he looks hungry?" she asked us. She told the bus driver to stop. She got off the bus and gave the man twenty dollars. She never could stand to see someone in need.

John was free-hearted about helping people out, even more than June. He reached out a hand to hundreds: people in the music business, people going through hard times, and people on his staff.

John backed a bunch of music people, both rising stars who needed a break and old-timers down on their luck. He helped a lot of people get ahead in the music business: Larry Gatlin, George Jones, Merle Haggard, the Statler Brothers, the Oak Ridge Boys, and Johnny Paycheck, all got support from the Man in Black.

People were always giving him tapes and sending them in the mail; John tried to listen to as many as he could.

One songwriter John thought a lot of was Kris Kristofferson. Kris's song "Sunday Mornin' Comin' Down" turned out to a big hit for John and got Kris started on a huge career. I heard Kris say more than once, "John kept me from being hungry many times."

Larry Gatlin also got his start in the business with John and June's help. June heard him singing at church; I believe it was Jimmy Snow's church, the Evangel Temple on Dickerson Pike in Nashville. (Jimmy is the son of Opry star Hank Snow and Maybelle's good friend Minnie.) Anyway, June carried John to hear him sing the next week and John ended up offering him a job. John asked Larry if he wanted to help out on a recording he was working on.

"I lost my job two days ago," Larry said. "I'll be there."

That turned into a lifelong friendship. He worked with John on several recordings and came by to see him and June quite a bit. They really missed him when he moved to Texas. John and June were godparents to Larry's son Josh Cash Gatlin.

Larry spoke at John's funeral, at one point talking directly to Josh: "Son, this man fed your mama and me when we couldn't afford food. He paid rent for us when we couldn't pay rent."

Music City newcomers weren't the only ones who got a helping hand.

A few years back, Johnny Russell (who wrote "Act Naturally," among many others) got support from John–

and from June, too, though she didn't know it at the time!

June was in the hospital again, and she had about fifteen hundred dollars in her purse. When John came by to see her, I told him he better take the money home with him.

It happened that Johnny Russell was in the hospital at the same time. He'd been having a terrible time with diabetes, and they'd had to amputate his legs.

"Peggy, Johnny Russell's over there in rehab," he told me. "Push me over to see him." As I rolled his wheelchair through the hallways John was straightening and counting June's bundle of money. He peeled off a thousand dollars and stuck it in his shirt pocket.

When we got to Johnny Russell's room, he was touched to see his old friend. John gave him the thousand bucks and said, "Son, I don't want you to think this is a handout. But I'd like you to have it if you think you can use it."

Well, Johnny was all tore up. He started to cry and said, "John, I can't take your money from you."

John gave him a solemn look. "It's okay," he said. "It's not my money; it's June's."

Well, we went back to June's room and John couldn't wait to tell her he'd given her money away. "Honey, who did you give it to?" was all she asked. He told her about Johnny Russell and she said, "Well, that's nice, honey. I guess he needs it."

To John and June, generosity wasn't just about hand-ing out money. Joe Maphis was a legendary guitar picker who influenced Chet Atkins and Merle Travis, among others. He played a double-necked guitar and wrote music for Hollywood westerns. When he died in 1986, his wife Rose Lee had no place to bury him. John had him buried at Woodlawn East (now called Hendersonville Memory Gardens) right by Maybelle. His son Dale died shortly afterwards, and John buried him right there with the Cash and Carter family, too.

John and June were good-hearted about another burial–at least what they thought was a burial. It started while we were on tour in Europe. After a show I got John and June settled in the hotel and went off to my room. I hadn't been there long when the phone rang.

"Honey, you've got to come back up here. Something has happened," June said. "Get Helen and Anita–we've got to pray about this."

I figured somebody had died.

We got up there and sure enough: Terry Rogers was dead.

June's daughter Rosey was divorced from Terry, who was Billy Joe Shaver's nephew. Billy Joe had written John's hit "Old Chunk of Coal." And Billy Joe's wife Brenda used to work at the House of Cash.

Anyway, Rosey had called June and told her Terry's poor body had been laying cold at the morgue for a week because nobody would claim it. We all talked it over and prayed, then John called the office and told them to give Rosey the money to get him buried.

Two years later our friend Pennilane was in Waco, Texas, visiting Billy Joe and Brenda. They invited her for dinner, and there sat Terry Rogers with his new wife and baby. Penni said she about passed out!

She told me the story when she got back. "He can't be alive," I said.

"Well, he can be and he is, because I just talked to him," Penni said.

I knew I'd have to tell John that Rosey had pulled another trick to get money. A few days later we were loading up the bus. June hadn't come out yet. "John, sit down," I said. "Terry Rogers is alive."

He just looked at me for a minute. "He can't be," he said. "Me and June buried Terry Rogers." He's alive, I insisted. "Can you prove that?" he asked me.

I told him Penni had gone to Waco and seen him. He just shook his head. "I'll tell you one thing, that's the biggest trick she ever pulled on me and June."

When he told June about it, she sighed and said, "I guess Rosey needed the money for something else."

That was the way June was: She wouldn't judge people. I can still hear her saying about somebody or other: "Just give him the benefit of the doubt." Whoever it was might have just killed somebody, but all June would say was, "Just give him the benefit of the doubt."

June never begrudged anybody. One time in Jamaica we came out of a store and there lay a poor man with one leg hollering and begging. June gave him some money and we went on down the street. It wasn't but a few minutes before we heard a ruckus and the man came running past us!

"Honey, isn't that the one-legged man we just gave money to?" she asked me. It didn't matter to June; she was just glad she could help him.

John and June loved their house in Jamaica, and they did everything they could to help the people there. Many of them are so poor they live in cardboard shacks with tree branches for a roof. June and John were always quick to respond when somebody needed help.

Sometimes it backfired.

The house in Jamaica had a big porch on each side of the house, and we used to spread out a tablecloth and eat there. One day, we noticed a bunch of children a few yards away in the woods. They were making a hand-to-mouth motion, and June told me to fix some food and carry it out to them.

The next day the same thing happened, only now there were more kids. Every day more and more came. The group got so big, finally June sighed and said, "I reckon we better just eat in the house from now on."

Whenever we drove anywhere, the children would run into the crosswalks and dance for money. John would always give them some. The Jamaicans really loved him. When he went into town they would flock around him, yelling, "Mr. Cash, Mr. Cash!"

It was always the kids that tugged at June's and John's hearts the most. They helped many, many children by supporting the SOS Children's Village near their home.

SOS Villages take in abandoned Jamaican children, who are cared for by homeless Jamaican women. Thousands of children have grown up at the Villages, many with the help of John and June. They did a lot of benefit concerts to raise money, and John's death notice requested donations be sent there.

And they did a lot of hands-on work, too. The last twelve or fifteen years, we'd go to Jamaica every year for the holidays. Before we left the States, June would send me out to Wal-Mart to buy gifts for the women and children at the Village. I'd get hundreds of pairs of shoes in all sizes, all kinds of clothes, socks and underwear, makeup kits, you name it. We'd rent a plane and load all that stuff on it, then fly down to Jamaica. When we delivered all the gifts, the kids would swarm around us like bees.

One little girl that touched their hearts had a club foot. John paid for three trips to the United States for her to have surgery.

June loved to give parties, and she made a special effort to find out if anyone in the Jamaica household was having a birthday. She'd throw them a party and buy some gifts for them to open. She loved bingo, just like her mama, and she'd hold bingo parties for the locals, giving away nice prizes like manicure kits and sets of dishes.

They were real kind to the staff at the Jamaica house, too. Desna was their housekeeper there for nearly thirty years. John brought her to the States for goiter surgery and then again for eye surgery.

Desna was the Jamaican housekeeper for nearly thirty years.

He also paid the whole staff very well. The usual pay in Jamaica is about ten dollars a day, but John always added an extra hundred dollars a week to their paychecks.

It wasn't just the Jamaica staff they took care of—everybody that worked for them received countless acts of generosity.

John sent a lot of the girls who worked for the House of Cash to college. He loved Israel, and at one time or another he took nearly every member of the staff there to visit.

In 2002, John received the National Medal of Arts in Washington, D.C. He took everybody with him: the band, his crew, the House of Cash and household staff, and his kids. He flew us all to Washington and put us up in a hotel. June bought me a four-hundred-dollar gown to wear to the presentation.

One of the more unusual gifts John gave his staff was plastic surgery. One day he came to us and said, "I'm giving all you girls a facelift if you want it, all expenses paid." Goldie Adcock, the wardrobe lady, and Winifred Kelley, who looked after John Carter, went to New York to get their work done. Hairdresser Pennilane went down to St. Petersburg. "Every time I look in the mirror I see the kindness and generosity of Johnny Cash," she said to me.

One time John and June told me they wanted to do something special for my sister Betty Hagewood. She'd been taking care of Mrs. Cash and they wanted to thank her.

I said, "John, she's never been out of the country. Why don't you take her on your next trip and I'll stay home?" Two weeks later Betty was on her way to England, Scotland, Germany, and Finland for three weeks. She had a blast.

Another time, we were in Jamaica and John said, "Peggy, get your sister on the phone for me."

I said, "John, it's only six o'clock back in Nashville, and Betty's still asleep."

He thought for a minute and decided we'd wait an hour. "I want to give Betty my Range Rover." He explained that Betty was the only one who would take care of it right.

June said, "Honey, that's so sweet."

"She deserves it," he said.

When he talked to her, he said, "I know they're expensive to take care of, so you can sell it if you want to. I don't care." She finally did sell it on the Internet a few years later.

After June died, John also gave her favorite .410 shotgun to Betty. And one night near the end he said, "Betty, bend over here." He was wearing three gold necklaces, and he took one off and put it on Betty's neck, just out of the blue.

John and June were always glad to do benefit concerts for good causes. Besides SOS Village, they did a concert at Opryland to benefit the police department and another concert for police officers' widows. One cause very close to their hearts was the Autistic Foundation, because June's sister Anita's son Jay is autistic.

John and June also helped a number of churches. When Jimmy Snow was raising money to build his Evangel Temple, John bought the vacant lot next door and donated it for a parking lot. He gave money to the Nashville Cowboy Church, founded by his sister Joanne and her husband. And when the new Catholic church in Hendersonville was vandalized, John sent a large donation to clean it up.

As they gave, so they received. John and June were overwhelmed by how much people thought of them. It seems like fans would give their last dollar to send John and June a present.

When Maybelle died, I went through the mail, and many people who loved her had sent thousands of dollars in cash—from singles to fifties and hundreds—for us to buy flowers.

At Christmas time the gifts would just pour in. Turkeys, hams, smoked chicken, candy, flowers, fruit, you name it. A lot came from record companies, music executives, and radio stations, but just plain folks sent presents too.

John told us to give everything to the staff or to people in need. "Except the country hams," he said. "We're not giving those away."

They always got dozens of flower arrangements when they were in the hospital. I'd carry them around to other patients and take the rest to nursing homes.

John and June treated me just like a member of their family for more than thirty years, and they always let me know how much they thought of me.

One day they called me in. John said, "Peggy, we need to talk to you."

I laughed. "What have I done now?" I asked.

"No, no," John said. "This is serious. You deserve a home, and we should have already given you one." They gave me the title to a house for what was left on the note, about nine thousand dollars. John's daughter Cindy was moving out, and they deeded it over to me. I'm still living there today.

"Honey, we have no idea what we'd do without you,"

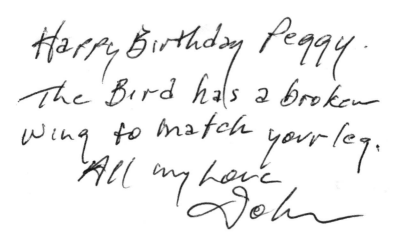

Harry Birthday Peggy.
The Bird has a broken
wing to match your leg.
All my Love
John

John gave me a very special birthday present.

June said. "Nobody has ever taken care of us like you have."

I was really touched. "I'll take care of y'all to the end of time," I promised.

Most of the time, though, it was just little presents here and there. Every time June went shopping she'd buy me and Betty shoes, clothes, makeup, you name it. John was the same way. I'd take him shopping and he'd ask, "What do you need? Get you something too."

For my fiftieth birthday, John said, "We're going to give you all fifty dollar bills." Sure enough, their birthday card held a thousand dollars in fifty dollar bills.

Another time, John said, "Peggy, you got a phone call, and I left the message by your bed." I didn't think much about that, until I saw the message. It was from John and June, and it said, "This is for all the good things you do for us." It had three thousand dollars in it!

One of my favorite gifts is a silver box that I keep on my dresser. On top is a bird with a broken wing. At the time, I was laid up with a bad knee–I'd hurt it playing softball and was hobbling around in a cast. It was my birthday, and John came in with a present. "I saw this in an antique store and it reminded me of you," he said.

I still have the card that came with it, which says, "Happy Birthday, Peggy. The bird has a broken wing to match your leg. All my love, John."

One day after June died, John was sitting in her bedroom missing her. He told me to go in her closet and get me some of June's clothes.

"June would want you to have them," he insisted. I picked out a couple of things, and John said, "Take more." I have a closet full of June's clothes that I cherish–dresses, shoes, furs, and evening bags–and some of her jewelry, including pins, earrings, and bracelets. June was a big girl, so the clothes mostly don't fit me, but I get them out every now and then because they remind me of her.

John also gave me my most treasured possession. A couple of weeks after June died, he asked me if I wanted something to remember her by. "Oh, John," was all I could say.

"How about one of her instruments?" he asked.

I thought immediately of June's autoharp. Maybelle had taught me to play the harp a little and I loved hearing both her and June play it.

I was a little scared to ask. "Is it okay for me to have her autoharp?"

He gave it to me right then and there. It was so sweet

and thoughtful of him to give me such a big piece of June's life. But that was John all over.

To this day I can see her sitting on the porch in Jamaica and hear her strumming "Wildwood Flower" on that harp. There's an awful lot of June left in it.

The Girls

BETWEEN THEM, JOHN and June had six daughters, and sixteen sons-in-law (including one who married two different daughters), two daughters-in-law, fourteen grandchildren, and three great-grandchildren.

It's hard to keep them straight without a scorecard, so you can read the genealogy at the end of this chapter.

June and John loved them to pieces, but all the kids—hers, his, and theirs—were a handful. John and June stayed busy trying to keep them out of trouble. June especially was always trying to take care of them, always sending money to help them out. There's no telling how much money they gave their children over the years.

I think John and June were trying to make up for all the time they spent away from the kids when they were young. They toured a lot, and it just wasn't practical to take the children along. I think John and June felt guilty about it, and the kids quickly learned to take advantage of that.

John and his first wife Vivian were married from 1954 to 1966. We never saw much of Vivian, although she did come to town for weddings and receptions and such. John once told me they fought the whole time they were together. She was jealous of his being on the road all the time.

They had four daughters: Rosanne, Kathy, Cindy, and Tara. One of the things John and Vivian fought about was the girls' names: He didn't want any of them to have a middle name, and Vivian did. Only Tara, the youngest, has one.

I first met Rosanne when she was touring with John and June and I was taking care of Maybelle. She's the only professional singer of John's children. Ironically, she once recorded one of her father's songs–"Tennessee Flat Top Box"–before she knew he wrote it.

Rosanne always made her own living and never asked her parents for anything, as far as I know. When she was married to Rodney Crowell, they lived here in Nashville and came by sometimes for dinner, and also for Thanksgiving and Christmas. She and her family came down to Jamaica a few times, too.

I met Rodney in Las Vegas. Maybelle and I were playing blackjack, and June brought him over and introduced him as Rosanne's new boyfriend. "See what you can do with him, Mama," she said.

I sized him up. "Are you country or rock 'n' roll?" I asked.

John's daughters Tara, Kathy, and Cindy

"Well, which would you prefer?" he shot back.

Maybelle stepped in at that point. "Oh, leave him alone, Peggy," she said. "They've been trying to settle that for forty years."

I think he was the nicest of John and June's sons-in-law. He was always down to earth. We still saw a lot of Rodney after he and Roseanne were divorced.

Kathy and I worked together at the House of Cash and Museum. She was a tour guide and also fulfilled mail orders. She has a big heart and was always kind to everyone. We still keep in touch. Kathy married Jimmy Tittle, who played bass for John and co-produced his album *Classic Cash.* John was an ordained minister, and he performed their wedding ceremony.

Cindy Cash sings with her dad.

Cindy worked for John for a time, doing hair and makeup. From time to time she'd join John on stage. She also worked in the gift shop at the House of Cash. John once told me she was just like her mom.

We used to do some things together. She was really into metal detecting. John had bought her a real nice one, and I got one too. We went all over Hendersonville with those things, but all we ever found was a few coins and some rings.

Cindy liked to fish, and I told her about a few of my favorite fishing holes. One time, she and a friend met me and my sister Betty out in Cumberland City near Dover and we caught a bunch of fish.

Cindy's second husband was Jack Routh, her stepsister Carlene's ex-husband. He was the double son-in-law. Her third husband was Marty Stuart, a guitarist in John's band. They were married about five years.

Tara was the youngest of John's girls. John once told me she never gave him any problems, never asked him for anything. She'd bring her family down to Jamaica for Christmas. John and June were not real big on playing with kids on the beach, so I took them.

June was married to country singer Carl Smith from 1952 until the mid-Fifties. Their daughter Carlene was born in 1955.

John called Carlene "Bubbles" because she was always bouncing around. She and Rosey lived with John and June while they were in junior high. She was a typical teenager, in the homecoming court and on the cheerleading squad, but she ran with a fast crowd. What I mostly remember is she had a lot of boyfriends. I couldn't meet them all; there were just too many!

She traveled and sang some with the Carter Sisters, but she always seemed to be getting in trouble. Carlene got married real young to Joe Simpkins and they had a daughter, Tiffany Anastasia. After that marriage broke up, Tiffany stayed with June a lot of the time. June used to say she felt Tiffany was more like a daughter to her than a granddaughter .

Carlene's second husband, musician Jack Routh,

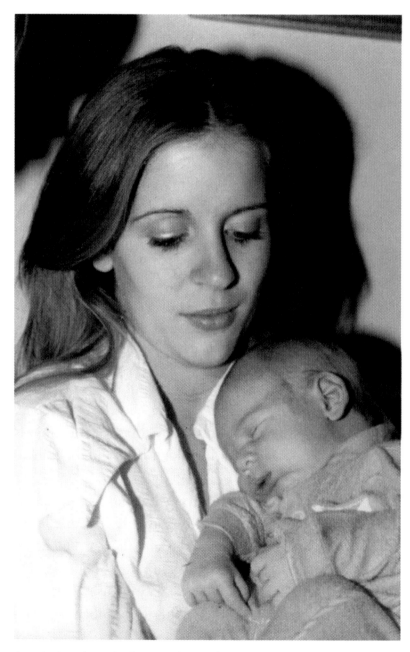

June's daughter Carlene and grandson John Jackson Routh

raised their son John Jackson Routh with little help from Carlene. At his college graduation John Jackson gave all the credit to his father and his stepmother. Carlene, as usual, got there late.

English rocker Nick Lowe was her third husband. After their divorce, Nick adopted and raised Carlene's daughter from her first marriage, Tiffany Anastasia.

June married Nashville policeman Rip Nix in 1957. Daughter Rosey was born in 1958.

What can I say about Rosey? I loved her to pieces, and I think she was probably June's favorite. She certainly had a special place in her heart. June called her "my little wildwood rose."

Rosey was a troubled soul.

She had a great big heart and was really kind. But she could be the best in the world or the worst.

She was the kind of person who would take from one person and turn around and give it to someone else. John used to say, "When you see Rosey doing something good, you better watch her because she's up to something." But she would do anything for anybody, even when she was messed up. If she had money, she would share it.

The other side of Rosey wasn't so nice. I remember we were on tour and I had my leg in a cast. One night a noise woke me up. Rosey patted me on the arm and told me to go back to sleep, that I needed my rest. I discovered later that in the hand behind her back she was holding half of my pain pills and fifty dollars I'd had in my purse.

Rosey, seen here with Dennis Devine, was June's "wildwood rose."

She had a lot of trouble with drinking and drugs, and was always wanting money. June tried to help her, but poor Rosey took advantage of that.

I remember one night June called my sister Betty at home. "Rosey's run off in a ditch and needs a hundred and twenty-five dollars to pay the tow truck driver," June said.

Betty jumped in her car, drove to Hendersonville to get the money from June, and then headed to Dickerson Pike in Nashville looking for Rosey. When she got to the place Rosey had described, there was no car in a ditch and no tow truck in sight.

Betty was about to drive off when she heard someone yelling from a filling station across the street. It was Rosey. She was fine; the car was fine; she'd just made up the story because she needed money.

Her father Rip Nix helped her out a lot. He gave her money until he found out what she was using it for. "I'm not giving you money to watch you kill yourself," he told her. "I'll give you my money when I'm gone." Of course, it turned out that he outlived her.

John and June took Rosey on tour with them, including a trip to Europe, in an effort to keep her straight. She sang "Amazing Grace" at every show and wowed the crowd. She had a beautiful voice; I think she sang the best of all Maybelle's grandchildren. She could write songs, too. It's a shame she wasted her talent.

June always thought Rosey would make it. "I believe Rosey's doing a little better today," she'd say. She could never accept what was clear to everybody else: that Rosey was a drug addict.

I last saw Rosey at John's funeral. She was really out of it, wandering up and down the aisle during the service. At one point she stopped and asked me how I was doing, the only family member who talked to me that day.

She called me a few weeks later from a payphone at RiverGate Mall just outside Hendersonville. "I want to thank you for taking care of my grandma and my mama and John all those years," she told me. "When I get my inheritance, the first person I'm going to give money to is you."

That was the last time I ever spoke to her. Drugs killed Rosey not three months after John died. She's laid to rest at June and John's feet.

John R. Cash

Born February 26, 1932, died September 12, 2003

    Married Vivian Liberto August 7, 1954 (divorced 1966)

        Rosanne Cash born May 24, 1955

            Married Rodney Crowell in 1979 (divorced 1991)

                Caitlin Rivers Crowell born 1980

                Chelsea Jane Crowell born January 25, 1982

                Carrie Kathleen Crowell born December 12, 1988

            Married John Leventhal April 30, 1995

                Jakob William Leventhal born January 22, 1999

        Kathleen (Kathy) Cash born April 16, 1956

            Married Thomas A. Coggins, 1972

                Thomas Gabriel Coggins born March 25, 1973

                Married Charisma

                    Brennan Coggins born September 15, 1997

            Married James A. (Jimmy) Tittle November 4, 1982

                James Dustin Tittle born July 12, 1984

                Kacy Rosanne Tittle born June 19, 1987

        Cynthia (Cindy) Cash born July 29, 1958

            Married Chris Brock January 14, 1977

                Jessica Dorraine Brock born July 22, 1977

            Married Jack Routh

            Married Marty Stuart March 31, 1983

            Married Eddie Panetta May 22, 2003

        Tara Joan Cash born 1961

            Married Fred Schwoebel June 30, 1991

                Aran Thomas Schwoebel born November 21, 1994

                Alexander Roland Schwoebel born

Valerie June Carter
Born June 23, 1929, died May 15, 2003

  Married Carl Smith July 9, 1952, divorced January 18, 1957

    Rebecca Carlene Smith born September 26, 1955

      Married Joe Simpkins, 1971

        Tiffany Anastasia Simpkins Lowe born 1971

        Luna Kai Darling born

      Married Jack Routh June 15, 1974

       John Jackson Routh born

        Married Emily Maddox

          Anita Grace Routh born February 13, 2003

      Married Nick Lowe, August 18, 1979

  Married Edwin "Rip" Nix November 11, 1957

    Rozanna Lea (Rosey) Nix born July 13, 1958;
    died October 24, 2003

      Married Scott Lawhead

      Married Mike Daniel

      Married Terry Rogers

      Married Phillip Adams 2002

  Married John R. Cash March 1, 1968

    John Carter Cash born March 3, 1970

      Married Mary Jaska June 14, 1995

        Joseph John Cash born February 25, 1996

      Married Laura Weber July 1, 2000

        Anna Maybelle Cash born July 8, 2001

The Son

IN MARCH 1970, John changed the traditional way he opened every show. Instead of saying, "Hello. I'm Johnny Cash," he opened his TV show by saying, "Hello. I'm . . . John Carter Cash's daddy!"

I was living with Maybelle when John Carter was born on March 3. The whole family was so excited because John and June had only girls.

Winifred Kelley, a nurse at Madison Hospital, took care of June and her newborn. When June started working again, Winifred left her job at the hospital to take care of John Carter at home and, when he got older, tutor him on the road.

John and June carried John Carter on every tour. He'd come out and take a bow. As he got older, he'd sing a couple of songs.

When he was old enough for kindergarten, I saw him nearly every day. John or June would take him to Goodpasture Christian School and pick him up in the afternoon.

John Carter started performing with his parents at an early age.

Whoever was driving would stop by Maybelle's house and visit with her and me. If they were working, I'd get him after school and bring him back to Maybelle's. We'd eat a snack and play games.

After Maybelle died and I started working for John and June, I was the one who drove John Carter around.

Despite living in the limelight, he was never really

spoiled. He was mostly a regular kid growing up. He made friends with a lot of the boys he went to school with. I took them to the movies all the time. John Carter loved roller-skating and I took them all to the rink. Sometimes we'd have skating parties.

Other times he'd invite his friends over for swimming parties. We'd grill hamburgers and roast marshmallows over at the Compound.

He was never into sports—he was kind of clumsy-like. But he was a fairly smart student. Plus, he traveled all over the world with his parents and learned a lot that way.

On tour, John put his son on the payroll. He'd come out and sing a song or two. He wasn't much of a singer; in fact, he got booed sometimes at John and June's concerts. I remember him coming backstage saying, "I don't want to go out there no more." John would just look at him and say, "Son, you've got to go back out there."

John Carter was always his daddy's boy, much closer to John than to June. In John's eyes, his son could do no wrong.

June was more realistic: She knew her son wasn't perfect, and he did some things she didn't care for. I heard them disagree about John Carter every so often, and John always won in the end. So when June saw John Carter do something wrong, she always left it to John to handle. And he wouldn't do anything.

John Carter loved the outdoors. He'd come down to the Florida house and go fishing with his dad. When he

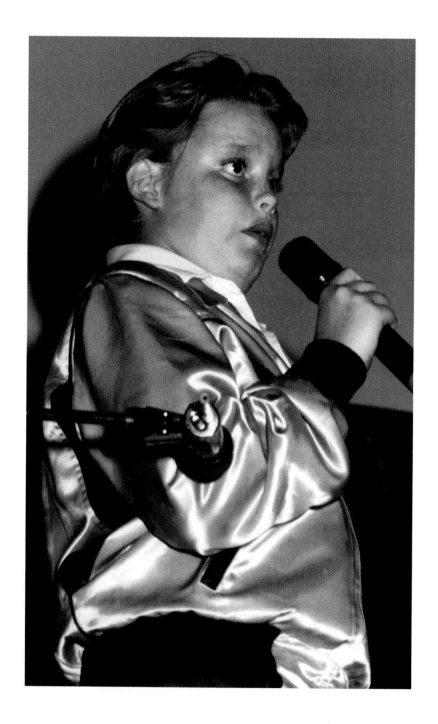

was in his teens, John and June would take him and me up to the Canadian wilderness for a vacation. We went every summer for several years.

We'd fly to Saskatchewan and climb in a seaplane. They'd take us two hundred fifty miles farther north and put us out by a lake with two Indian guides.

We were about as far away from everything as you can go. It was very primitive. We slept in bunk beds in a tiny old cabin. The men and women would take turns bathing in the ice-cold lake. For dinner, the guides cleaned the fish we caught and cooked them on sticks over the wood fire. We'd pack the rest of the fish in dry ice to take back to Tennessee.

June and I would go out on the lake in a canoe with one guide and John and John Carter went with their guide in another. One time June caught a twenty-six pound Northern pike. When she hooked it, she started hollering so loud it scared one of the guides and he came rushing back to shore. June took that fish home and had it mounted.

In those days, John Carter wore a retainer. One night after dinner, John Carter missed his retainer, and we couldn't find it anywhere. Finally, at about one a.m. I guessed that he'd wrapped it in a napkin and it had been thrown out when we cleared the table.

I got out of bed and walked through the woods to where the trash had been dumped. The bears had been in it and scattered garbage everywhere. But I dug through it, and kept digging until I found the retainer. Everybody was

A proud dad backs up his son.

amazed, not only that I'd found it, but that I'd even gone looking for it in all that trash in the first place.

When he was older John Carter started showing more interest in music. John turned the lakeside round room into a music room with a piano and a drum set. John

Carter got a couple of bands together, playing locally in Nashville and down in Florida. Later he played guitar and sang backup for John and June on the road. When they quit touring, he started working in the studio, producing records.

When he got married, he and his wife moved into Mrs. Cash's old house. His wife's name was Mary, and they named their son, born in 1996, Joseph John Cash. John called them the holy family: John, Mary, and Joseph.

John Carter is as big as his father but favors his mom.

It had been a long time since John and June had a young child around. They played with Joseph just like they were children too.

Christmas
at the Cashes

APART FROM JOHN Joseph, John and June never got to see their other grandchildren much. They'd send them birthday gifts every year, but that was about it. Kathy once told me, "My kids hardly know their grand-daddy." But many of the children lived out of town, and John and June were always away from home a lot.

The one time they did get to see kids and grandkids was at Christmas time in Hendersonville.

June went all-out decorating the house at Christmas time. The lakefront round room in Hendersonville was the center of activities, with a huge tree and hundreds of dec-orations. For several years, John and June used only orna-ments and decorations sent by their fans.

Before the big event, we'd shop for two or three weeks straight. I'd take June shopping, and then John would want me to take him. After that they'd shop together for the kids. Then John would get special gifts for his kids, and June would do the same for hers.

They both loved to buy gifts. Of course, June would shop at the drop of a hat, but John really got into Christmas shopping too.

On Christmas Eve, everybody gathered for a party. The kids and grandkids all came, including Rodney Crowell and his girls even after he was divorced from Rosanne. I'd make a big dinner: turkey and dressing, green beans, mashed potatoes, Silver Queen corn (June's favorite), sweet potatoes, deviled eggs, and cornbread. For dessert I always made John's favorite, coconut cake decorated with candy canes and gumdrops.

After we ate, we'd all head for the round room. John and June would pull the gifts from under the tree, calling out names. It was always a huge pile of presents; everybody got more than one.

John loved getting presents, much more than June did. His favorites were framed pictures of the grandkids and candy. He loved chocolate, and June would buy him pounds of See's Candy whenever we were in New York.

Then it was time for the Hot Seat. One family tradition was the Hot Seat. Anytime there was a gathering–at Christmas, a party, or just a bunch of friends together for one of John's guitar pulls–they'd put a chair in the middle of the room. That was the Hot Seat.

John would point to everybody in turn; they'd have to sit in the chair and either tell a story or sing a song. Everybody had a great time and a lot of laughs. Sometimes the Hot Seat sessions would go on half the night, five or six hours at a stretch.

Their special friends got candy and flowers. They'd send flowers to people they loved like the Gatlins, Willie Nelson, Robert Duvall, June's old friend Rosemary, and June's family back in Virginia like Janette, Fern, Rita, and Sue Hensley.

I wrapped the presents John gave, and he wrote the tags himself. I remember he and I went out in Jamaica one year. He said, "Peggy, let's go shopping. I want to buy something for June for Christmas."

He bought her a real nice Swiss watch and we went on to another store. He found a beautiful diamond-studded watch and decided he'd buy it for June, too.

I reminded him that he'd already bought June a watch, but he bought it anyway.

We got back to the house and I wrapped both watches. He filled out the tags, as usual, and when he gave me the packages back, he'd put my name on the Swiss watch. It's still a treasure to me.

Cashland

JOHN AND JUNE owned quite a bit of real estate. Besides the house, the Compound, Mrs. Cash's house, and the House of Cash in Hendersonville, there was Maybelle's house in Madison, the Mountain House, the farm in Bon Aqua, houses in Florida and Jamaica, the Carter homeplace in Virginia, and apartments in New York and New Jersey.

John bought the Hendersonville house while it was still under construction in 1967. The owner had traveled all over Tennessee and Kentucky buying up hand-cut barn timbers a hundred years old and used them in a huge house built on the bank of Old Hickory Lake.

The house was still under construction when John and June got married. But she started right in on fixing it up— and kept on fixing it until it was wall-to-wall furniture. For a while it was like going into a castle.

You could enter from the back through a foyer on the third floor. The master bedroom area is on the left with

John's office, June's sitting room, and their bathrooms. To the right are John Carter's room and the White Bedroom.

The main entrance was really in the back of the house, facing the lake. Steps on either side of the house lead down to the second floor and the main entrance.

The house has two-story, thirty-five-foot round rooms at each end. On the second floor is the Blue Room, one of the round rooms. The other round room is a music room, which has a round bed. Between them are the large den, kitchen, and a dining room that seats ten. A room with a big pool table is also on this floor.

The first level has two round sunrooms with wood-burning stoves. There are two huge dining rooms on the first floor, plus a half kitchen.

At ground level is a laundry room and a double garage where June kept her Rolls-Royce. Originally, the swimming pool was near the garage but kept getting run-off from the road. John had it filled in, and June turned it into a garden. They built a new pool up by the third level.

The Compound was across the street from the house. Originally a hundred forty-six acres, John sold all but about fifty acres. A log home on the property was set up as a recording studio.

The grounds were stocked with deer, turkeys, chickens, pigs, horses, goats, llamas, and peacocks. John liked having animals that were different, so he got a flock of emus as well as some Araucana chickens. These funny-

John liked unusual animals. These emus could be mean birds.

looking birds without a rump were so pampered their feet never touched dirt. Their feathers were soft as fur.

Originally introduced from Chile, the Araucana chickens laid green and blue eggs, reportedly cholesterol-free. They tasted like regular eggs to me.

A pair of buffalo roamed the Compound for a while, but one day the male rooted John Carter's pet pig into the ground and killed it. John was afraid they'd hurt somebody, so he had them slaughtered and we ate them. The meat was excellent. I grilled some steaks, made a roast, and John used some in his famous chili.

He got the heads stuffed and hung them in the House of Cash museum.

John bought the House of Cash building from the owners of a dinner theater that closed. He turned the stage area into the museum and the lobby became the gift shop. The second floor housed the business offices.

I started working for John in the House of Cash gift shop.

The museum displayed lots of clothes, including many of June's and John's stage outfits. It had the iron bed John used as a child and one of June's canopy beds. June contributed mementos and instruments from the Carter family. Awards and gold records won by John, June, and the Carters lined the walls along with photographs of family members and stars.

The gift shop stocked everything related to the Cash and Carter families: compact discs, tapes, and records; T-shirts and hats; key chains, coffee mugs, pencils, and pens with their pictures on them; headbands, bandanas, and hat pins; and John's and June's books.

Also on the property was the Amqui Station Antique Store, where June sold the antiques she didn't have room for. It had dishes, beds and other furniture, old pictures and frames, and jewelry—much of it bought when John and June went antiquing in Nashville and on tour.

The House of Cash was a real family affair. Besides his mom, who worked in the gift shop, John's sister Reba managed the House of Cash, and her daughter Kelly worked there handling the mail.

They'd get boxes and boxes of mail. It came to the house; it came to the House of Cash; every once in a while the Grand Ole Opry would send over a boxful that had come to them. Mail even came to a house Maybelle hadn't lived in for years.

In 1995 John finally got tired of fooling with the museum and gift shop and closed them down.

* * *

Maybelle's old singing partner Sara Carter visited her regularly in the Due West house.

I lived with Maybelle in her home on Due West Avenue in Madison. It had originally been June's house when she was married to Carl Smith in the early 1950s. Sometime later June also bought the property next door.

After Maybelle's death, June was approached about building a retirement home on the next-door property. She donated the land in exchange for lifetime ownership of a two-bedroom apartment in the new center. She later gave the apartment back to the center, now known as the Maybelle Carter Senior Adult Community.

John bought his parents a house in Hendersonville. After Mrs. Cash died, John gave the house to John Carter, who lived there with his first wife.

In 2002 John Carter called his parents and told them he was going to sell the house. June said, "We don't want just anybody living there. Let me let you talk to your daddy."

When John got off the phone, he said, "I can't believe our son wants to sell us this house, after we gave it to him." John Carter had told him if they didn't buy it he was going to sell it to someone else.

John and June had given it to him free and clear, and they ended up buying it back from him!

The Mountain House outside Hendersonville in the Tyree Springs community was built from great big logs. It was originally one of three cabins—the other two were later sold. The Mountain House was very private, sitting way up on a hilltop. John and June went there when they wanted to get away for a while.

John had quite a few acres on a farm in Bon Aqua, about forty miles southwest of Nashville. He had a vineyard there, and he and I would go down to trim the grapevines. In the later years when he couldn't stand up, he'd sit in a chair and tell me how to prune.

Every so often John "needed to get away from the world," as he put it, by himself. He headed for Bon Aqua.

I'd cook a pot of beans and go to the store to stock up on bread, onions, cheese and crackers, crunchy peanut butter, thick bologna, bananas, oatmeal (which he cooked himself), and ice cream, mostly chocolate.

John planted this grape arbor at the Bon Aqua farm.

June bought her old family homeplace and restored it.
She planted plenty of her favorite flowers.

Then I'd take him down there and leave him. None of us was ever sure what all he did there. He'd mess with the grapevines, pruning them and taking cuttings and sticking them in the ground. He'd go hunting squirrels and rabbits. He'd sit on the porch swing and write some songs, go fishing for brim and bluegill, and make a mess, mostly.

We'd call him every day and go down to check on him once or twice. He always greeted us with "Girls, I've got a big mess for you." Dirty plates were just stacked in the sink, and there'd be fish guts everywhere from where he tried to clean his catch. Betty would cook the fish for him, then we'd clean up his mess and leave him to himself until he was ready to come home.

* * *

They also owned the farm where June grew up. When Maybelle and Mr. Carter moved to Nashville, they sold the homeplace to his brother Grant and Grant's wife Theta. After Grant died, Aunt Theta sold the farm to June. It's now on the National Register of Historic Places.

John loved visiting Virginia as much as June did.

A trip to Virginia meant visiting with relatives. June's cousins Fern and Flo dropped by to see June.

In addition to the big house, June bought a little house down in front of the road that had belonged to June's aunt's sister. The third house on the property was a little white house up in the woods, not too far from the main house. June's cousin Nell and her husband Ford McConnell took care of the place for them.

Ladies in Waiting

JUNE ALWAYS LIKED to have a lot of people around—I think that's why she had so many people working for her. There were four of us she called her "Ladies in Waiting": Anna Bisceglia, my sisters Shirley Huffines and Betty Hagewood, and me. John just called us "the girls."

June was a great boss. Every year she'd throw a birthday party for each of us: lunch or dinner, a birthday cake, and a present each from John and June. They each liked to give a gift they'd picked out themselves.

John and June always treated us like family, not employees. They never left us out when they had a party. And there was always a place at the table—we were welcome to eat with them any time we wanted.

June never asked you to do anything without saying "Honey" first, and she always said "thank you" when you finished. Many times she told me, "I'd never ask any of you to do something I wouldn't do myself." We all worked hard for her.

The "Ladies in Waiting" were Anna Bisceglia, Shirley Huffines, Betty Hagewood, and me.

Anna was hired to do housework around 1970. She was also the one to polish all of June's silver—and there was an awful lot of it. June wanted it cleaned at least once a month so it would always be shiny.

Every once in a while Anna would cook an authentic Italian meal for John and June, and every Easter she made them her favorite Easter bread.

Anna's husband Armando was head of security. His brother-in-law built the Hendersonville house.

My sister Betty worked for John and June for seventeen years. She started out at the House of Cash, then June wanted her to come do housework. She also ran errands, took John and June shopping, and tended the garden.

She and I alternated working weekends so one of us

was always on hand. At the end, when John was at his weakest, he was a still big man, and it took two people to manage him. Betty helped me bathe him, take him to the bathroom, help him get around, and push his wheelchair.

John always said, "If we ever needed someone to fight for us, we'd want Betty. She could take care of them."

Shirley was in charge of washing and ironing for eleven years. Clothes, sheets, pillowcases, tablecloths, and napkins: June wanted everything pressed but the towels. And she liked fresh linens on the table every day, so there was always a lot to wash and iron. If she ever got caught up, Shirley would help around the house, but that didn't happen too often.

Every year June threw a nice birthday party for each of us.

* * *

I grew up in the Bordeaux part of Nashville, the eighth of twelve children. I was only seven when my parents divorced and I began a lifetime of helping out.

My mama did what she could to feed the family: taking in ironing and picking vegetables to be sold at the Farmers Market. My sisters and I helped out in the fields, picking onions, lettuce, cauliflower, tomatoes, and beans.

I left high school at sixteen so I could help support my family. My favorite teacher, Louise Pierce, had a five-year-old son; I took care of him and did some cooking and cleaning. After fifty years, Louise and I are still close friends.

At one point I even sold concessions at the Sulphur Dell baseball park in Nashville to make some money.

All that didn't leave much time for fun, but I loved listening to country music on the radio (even though my sisters made fun of me) and I played bingo with my girlfriends.

And one night there sat Maybelle Carter. I've never met a stranger in my whole life, so naturally Maybelle and I got to talking. One thing led to another, and almost before I knew it I'd been helping out the Carter and Cash families for more than thirty years as a "Lady in Waiting."

A Day in the Life

JOHN AND JUNE never lived the glamorous life of a couple of stars. They were as down to earth as anybody in the world. At heart they were good country people.

They both got up with the sun—or before. I'd get to the house about six in the morning, and they would already have been up for an hour or two, watching CNN, reading *The Tennessean* (June would check the ads to see what was on sale), and drinking coffee.

John loved strong coffee. He ordered Kona coffee from Hawaii: Twelve pounds at forty-nine dollars a pound were delivered once a month. He'd drink three or four cups in the morning and a couple more at night. That stuff was so strong it would knock you down. June stuck to regular brands from the grocery store. If she drank the Kona she'd water it down with milk.

By the time I got there, they'd usually decided what they wanted to do that day. It might be shopping—they both really liked to shop—or fishing, or visiting friends, or just staying home.

I'd make some breakfast about eight or so and we'd be ready to go.

If shopping was on the agenda, likely as not we'd go to Wal-Mart. They both loved that place. If June found a housedress she liked, she'd buy one in every color. John was the same way. He'd buy ten pairs of cotton lounging pants at a time, even though they were too short for him. June made fun of his "highwaters," as she called them. The Man in Black liked loud colors unless he was onstage.

June would buy thirty pairs of shoes at a time, sizes six to ten. She loved to give them away. If you did something special for her, she'd say, "Honey, pick out some shoes. There's bound to be a pair to fit you."

She also loved Stein Mart. If linens were on sale, we'd be there for hours.

John liked to go to the grocery store with me. He'd hop in one of those electric carts and take off down the aisles, knocking stuff off left and right with me right behind him picking them up.

At one time, my nephew sacked groceries at Kroger and John always made sure we got in his line—and gave him a big tip.

I'd take him to Lowe's and he'd buy stuff we didn't even need, light bulbs and screwdrivers and such. He always thought he needed to buy a hammer. I'd tell him, "John, you've got plenty of hammers." But that didn't stop him. I bet he had more than a hundred of them. He was

Either I helped June in the kitchen or she helped me.

June took this picture of John and me in Jamaica. We'd been playing dominoes—you can see the scoresheet on the table.

just as bad about flashlight batteries. He probably had enough batteries to light up every flashlight in Hendersonville!

Wherever we went, including Lowe's, they'd both insist on buying me something too. "Peggy, get yourself something," they'd say. "What do you need?"

We'd head back to the house for lunch, usually just a snack or salad. After lunch John would take his nap; June would read or piddle around the house.

With so many kids and friends, you'd never know who might be dropping by for a visit. They were always delighted to see everybody. If it was near dinnertime, John would insist that they stay to eat.

We'd have supper about four-thirty, just like country folks. (If people were coming over, we called it dinner.)

John finally beat me at dominoes: You can tell by his smiley face.

John and June ate in one of the dining rooms every night. The table was always set with some of June's fine linens, crystal, china, and silver. Sometimes they sat at each end of the long table, sometimes both at one end.

They never served alcohol in the thirty-three years I was with them. Once in a while a couple would bring a bottle of wine to dinner. Occasionally, June would have half a glass and John a full one. But they were nearly tee-totalers, in spite of all the rumors to the contrary.

Sometimes they tried to eat healthy. One time they got on a carrot juice kick. They kept me busy fetching them carrot juice until they both turned orange!

Every once in a while John and June would tell me they were going on a diet. They'd have a salad for dinner one night, but by the next day they'd go back to eating whatever they wanted. They did cut back on salt and sugar when John was diagnosed with diabetes.

After we ate, John would pick up a guitar and play a little. June—and Maybelle when she was alive—would sing along.

At night we'd play card games or dominoes. John and I would play dominoes for hours at a time, and he was really competitive. One night June pulled me aside and said, "Honey, you've just got to let John win or I'm going to have to run away from home."

She told me he came up to bed mad as a bear when he lost. "I can't win," he would say. "I'm just going to quit playing." Or he wouldn't talk at all.

"He's getting real hard to live with," she said.

Well, that night I fixed it so he'd win, and he was happy. "Well, I beat her tonight!" he reported to June.

They didn't watch a lot of television, but they loved "The Sopranos." They made sure they didn't miss an episode. I didn't watch it much because they were always talking nasty. Sometimes we'd watch a new-release movie— June's best friend Rosemary, her roommate while she was at acting school in New York, sent us movies that weren't even in theaters yet.

John loved westerns, but June was partial to murder mysteries. We'd be watching along and she'd say, "Be quiet, they're gonna get him, they're gonna get him." John would say, "Oh, June, they can't hear you." All she'd say was "You hush!"

Late in the evening, John would often go to his office off the master bedroom. He'd lie down on the half-bed and watch some television (mostly CNN and the Weather Channel), go to sleep for a while, wake up and watch a little more, then go to bed.

June usually went to her room around eight-thirty or nine, where she'd watch TV and read. She was always waking up the next morning with her glasses on her nose and a book on her chest.

When they went to bed, I'd finish cleaning up from dinner and head for home. Then at six the next morning we'd start all over again.

Fast Cars, Fast Women

JUNE HAD A whole fleet of cars that she drove depending on her mood. Every once in a while, she'd pipe up, "Let's go to McDonald's and get an ice cream cone. Get out the Rolls-Royce."

And off we'd go in her powder-blue Rolls. I don't imagine the McDonald's drive-thru sees all that many Rolls-Royces. June would pull up and order, then she'd always say, "Look out, here we come."

Of course, they knew who it was, and the kids would be cracking up when we got to the window.

June liked to drive fast, so she got a red Ferrari just like Tom Selleck's. She absolutely loved it. That thing would fly, too. One time she carried me to a funeral and on the way home she had it up to a hundred and thirty miles per hour on the Interstate. "Slow down, slow down," I said. "We're both going to get a ticket."

She laughed and said, "Oh, honey, I just wanted to show you what it would do."

You didn't see many Ferraris in Hendersonville, and June attracted attention. One day she had just passed the Bluegrass Market when she saw a man drive into a telephone pole. Being June, of course she stopped to see if he was okay.

"It wasn't your fault," he said. "I was busy looking at your car."

She had a black Mercedes, too. We were riding around one time and June started telling me how she used to drive with her feet when she was a kid.

"With your feet?" I said. I didn't know what in the world she was talking about.

"Yeah, watch this." She put her feet up on the steering wheel and away we went. (She was really limber, I guess from dancing and carrying on onstage.)

"June, you're going to kill us both," I yelped. She just laughed and kept going.

John had a black Mercedes and a silver one, which I think was the only car he ever owned that wasn't black. The black Mercedes had a big old engine in it. When you'd hit the gas at a stoplight that thing would raise right up off the ground. This tickled John Carter when he was a kid.

"Step on it, Peggy," he'd say.

"Oh, I can't do that, John Carter," I'd tell him.

"Step on it!" he'd command and off we'd go like a dragster.

One time John drove the silver Mercedes over to the Compound across the road from his house in Henderson-

This may be the only car John ever owned that wasn't black.

ville. For some reason he was driving it through a field and got stuck in the mud. John could be bull-headed some-times, and he was just determined to drive that car out of the mud.

Well, he kept at it, revving the motor and spinning his wheels. The longer he was stuck the harder he tried to get out. He kept putting the gas to it until the engine burned out.

John was a pretty rough driver. He'd sling you all around the car. He'd always hit the gas pedal and let up, hit the gas and let up, until you were about seasick, all the while driving fast as he could.

June would say, "Honey, you're going too fast." John would just laugh and keep going.

One time he nearly scared me to death. We were in Lake Tahoe and he wanted to go to the drugstore.

"I'll drive," he said. Traffic was always pretty bad in this little town. We came up on a traffic jam but that didn't stop John.

The next thing I knew he had two wheels up on the sidewalk. We went for three or four blocks with me saying the whole way, "We're gonna get it for this."

John said not to worry. "They know me out here." But when we were done shopping he said, "I guess you better drive back."

One of John's hits was called "One Piece at a Time." It tells of an assembly-line worker in Detroit who smuggled out a Cadillac in his lunchbox, one piece at a time. Well, he had a hard time putting it together right: The back only had one tailfin, there were three headlights, two on one side and one on the other, and when they tried to bolt it together all the holes were gone.

It was a clever song, and it inspired Bill Patch, a coal miner from Oklahoma. He actually built a one-piece-at-a-time car according to the lyrics, with the single tailfin and three headlights and all. Every part he used came from a different year, starting with 1949. He gave it to John, who put it on display at the House of Cash.

Stella Bays and I in front of the One-Piece-at-a-Time Car

That car sure was sure a sight. John named it The Cottonmouth and had a name plaque made for the car. Every morning we parked it out in front of the House of Cash and kept it in the basement at night. I'd drive it down to the service station to get it gassed up and the oil changed. You should have seen the looks on people's faces as I sailed by.

They used the car to make a really funny music video. You see John and June driving down the road in this crazy car. June's a-fussing, and John stops and puts her in the trunk! As he's closing the lid June starts hollering. She jumps out and takes off across a field.

John reaches in the trunk and pulls out a snake and beats it with a stick. The joke was, John's character knew it was just a rubber snake and was putting on a show.

John gave the car to Bill Patch's son a few months before June died.

Maybelle always drove a big old black Cadillac. Her husband had a string of Mercedes. Mr. Carter would drive crazy. Maybelle told me she always rode in the back seat when he drove. "But I spent more time in the floorboards than I did on the seat," she laughed.

Maybelle and I were always having adventures. One time we were on our way back to Madison about one in the morning. We'd been out playing poker with my brother Jimmy. Maybelle was telling me to hurry up because she had to go to the bathroom.

Just as I got off the Interstate a policeman pulled me over for not dimming my lights. I explained that Maybelle's Cadillac dimmed its lights automatically. I guess he didn't like that because he asked me to step out of the car.

He looked me up and down. The next thing I know, he's asking me if I've been drinking and I'm walking the yellow line.

Well, I hadn't been, and I walked the line just fine. He finally gave me a ticket for the headlights and let us go.

Back at home I let Maybelle out of the car and pulled it into the garage. As I was walking back to her she was just a-dying laughing. "What's so funny?" I asked, but she was laughing too hard to tell me.

Finally she said, "No wonder that policeman thought you'd been drinking. Look at your pants."

One leg of my pants was stuck down in my knee-high hose just below my knee. That cop probably thought I was too drunk to dress right.

It *was* quite a sight. I had pulled down my knee-highs while we were playing poker 'cause they were too tight. When we went to leave I yanked them back up but I got my pants leg stuck inside. That's the one and only time I ever had to walk the line.

June got off better than I did. They had a white truck we used at the farm. One time we'd been to Wal-Mart to buy shrubs and June ran a stop sign in the Riverchase subdivision.

A cop pulled her over and June started talking ninety miles a minute. He finally just let her go. June could talk her way out of anything.

Friends

JUNE AND JOHN loved having guests in their home, and a steady stream of friends came to visit. You never knew who would drop by, but you could be sure that they all loved John and June.

Ronnie Dunn was new in town when we first met him. He'd won a songwriting contest in Oklahoma, and the prize included a recording session in Nashville. He and his wife came out to the house because Janine Dunn was old friends with John and June—she'd been married to the late Bill Patch, who built the One-Piece-at-a-Time Car.

I was staying with Anita at the time, and she suggested we have the Dunns over for breakfast. John Schneider was in town and Anita invited him along with his mom and grandmother. Donna and Joe Spence also came over, and I cooked a big breakfast for all of them.

After we ate they started playing. Donna played a mean saxophone, and Ronnie and John played guitar. Then Ronnie sang one of the songs he won the contest with, "Boot Scootin' Boogie." That may have been the first time it was ever played in Nashville. The song turned out to be as good as we thought it was that morning.

George Jones had been friends with John ever since they both appeared on "Louisiana Hayride" in the mid-Fifties. He and his wife Nancy usually came to John and June's big parties. I met Nancy several times when George and John were on the same concert bill. She came to help out in George's souvenir booth right next to ours, and we visited between sales.

June knew George since their Grand Ole Opry days—she always called him her "little pal" and her "little possum." And she was very close to Tammy Wynette, who was married to George in the early Seventies.

George Jones was friends with John for many years.

Marty Stuart played in John's band.

Marty Stuart played guitar in John's band and married his daughter Cindy. He later went out on his own and divorced Cindy, but remained a very close friend. He called me "Aunt Peggy." I always teased Marty that you could count on him to show up at dinnertime.

Marty saw singer Connie Smith in concert when he was twelve years old. He came home and told his mama, "Someday I'm going to marry that woman." Twenty-five years later, he did! We saw them a lot after they bought the house next door in Hendersonville.

John always said that Connie was the most beautiful woman in the world—besides June. It was another friend of theirs, though, that really caught his eye.

Emmylou Harris was a very good friend. She came to visit whenever she was in town, and she sang at both their funerals. John always said, "If something ever happened to June, I believe I would have to go for Emmylou."

Roy Orbison lived next door to John. He and John toured together back in the early days and they remained good friends. Roy's life was filled with tragedy: His first wife was killed when they were out riding motorcycles. A couple of years later, his Hendersonville house burned down, and two of his three children died in the fire. Roy started a new family, and John Carter was big friends with a couple of his kids. Roy was only fifty-two years old when he died of a heart attack.

John later took Roy's oldest son, Wesley, on a European tour, where he made his first singing appearance in England. He sings just like his daddy.

Faron Young was another good friend of John's from way back. He loved the lake house and always said he wanted his ashes spread at John's place.

After Faron's funeral in 1996, his son Robin called John and asked if they could come out to the house and sprinkle his ashes on the lake. John and June were out of town, and John asked me to open the house and make them some breakfast.

They ate and we all went down to the shore. They said a prayer and slung some of the ashes in the lake. They threw some more up on the bank. John and June later had a plaque made for the bank that said "Faron Young Garden."

Some time later John and I were sitting on the dock fishing. John suddenly turned around and said out of the blue, "Hey, Faron, how you doing today?"

He laughed and said, "Old Faron might be out there watching me. I better behave."

In the early Nineties a fellow named Rick Rubin came into John's life. He owned a record label, American Recordings, and was a record producer—of rap and heavy metal groups. But he liked John's music and wanted to record him.

They recorded all over the place, at Rick's studio, at John's, and at an old church in California. John needed help walking for that session, so I took him and helped him

Fan Dennis Devine, second from right, poses with The Highwaymen: Kris Kristofferson, John, Waylon Jennings, and Willie Nelson.

get around. I got to sit and listen while they recorded–the church had a wonderful organ.

Whenever they recorded here in town, Rick would come out to the house for a few days. He and John would talk and pray together.

They ended up making several albums, and John always gave Rick credit for reviving his career.

Of all the friends who shared good times, June's favorites were a group she called her "babies"–Larry Gatlin, Waylon Jennings, Kris Kristofferson, Willie Nelson, and Hank Williams Jr.

June discovered Larry singing at church and John helped him break into the business. Larry did shows with John from time to time and often came to his concerts. He was a frequent drop-in visitor at the house.

Waylon and John also went way back: They were always getting into trouble in those days. John told me one time he and Waylon painted their whole hotel room black including the beds and curtains.

They shared an apartment before June came into the picture. John told me the place was always filthy because neither one of them was much on keeping house.

Later in life, they also shared a hospital stay. They were in Baptist Hospital at the same time on the same floor. One of them was always heading for the other's room, dragging his IV pole behind him.

Waylon had a Fifties Party to celebrate his fiftieth birthday. Most of June's "babies" were there wearing 1950s clothes. Willie was wearing some goofy round glasses with windshield wipers attached. Anita and our friend Donna Spence made matching poodle skirts. We rented a 1954 car to drive to Waylon and Jessi's house.

Waylon and John toured later with Kris and Willie as The Highwaymen.

Kris was another one of those who always seemed to come around about dinner time. John and June absolutely loved him, and vice versa. Kris named one of his kids after John. He is such a kind, gentle man. He cried the whole time at their funerals.

If Willie was in the neighborhood, he always dropped by to see John. They had known each other for such a long time. John made several appearances at Willie's Farm Aid concerts.

June took this photo of John and me with Waylon Jennings.

Once Willie heard on television that John was in Jamaica playing golf and sent him a set of golf clubs. Well, John had never played in his life. But for a month or so he'd get out the clubs and hit balls I found in the yard from the golf course next door. His interest in golf didn't last long and we left the clubs in Jamaica.

Hank Jr. was another "baby" that they dearly loved. I remember one time he sent John and June a Big Mouth Billy Bass, that singing fish you hung on the wall. When you walked up to it, their fish sang "Ring of Fire."

June was Hank Jr.'s godmother. She had known his dad Hank Sr. pretty well and was best friends with his wife Audrey.

John and June had probably a dozen godchildren. Roy Orbison asked them to be godparents for a couple of his children. Kris's son John, Jane Seymour's son John, and

Willie Nelson dropped by to visit every once in a while.

We're backstage at a concert. John holds his namesake, Kris Kristofferson's son. That's Kris's wife Lisa on the left.

the four children of friends John and Michelle Rollins were also godchildren.

June took being a godmother seriously: She always tried to send each of them something on their birthdays.

John and June both did some acting in their careers, and were friends with a lot of actors.

Jane Seymour and husband James Keach were frequent visitors. They even made special trips to visit John and June in the hospital.

They were some of the most down-to-earth people I

June and Robert Duvall were very good friends.

ever met. No wonder John and June liked them so. Especially Jane. She was raised poor, she told me once; she never got above her raising.

June met her on the set of her show "Dr. Quinn Medicine Woman," when June played Sister Ruth. They became great friends, getting into giggling fits during tapings. John also made several guest appearances, playing gunslinger Kid Cole.

Jane named her twin boys for John and for Christopher Reeve. When they were babies, Jane would lug one in each arm, "getting her exercise," she laughed. Baby John was a real handful, grabbing Big John by the nose when he got the chance.

Bobby Duvall was one of June's oldest and closest friends. They met in New York in the 1950s when June was taking acting lessons from famous director Elia Kazan.

June loved to tell a story from when she and Bobby were making the movie *The Apostle*. She played Duvall's mother in the movie. In the last scene, her character is lying in a casket. While they were filming, June suddenly sat bolt upright! Everybody fell out laughing.

June's roommate in New York was Rosemary Edelman, who became her very best friend. Rosemary loved my cornbread and biscuits so much I'd FedEx two big skillets of cornbread to her in Los Angeles. She swore it was still warm when she got it the next day.

John Schneider from the TV show "The Dukes of Hazzard" dropped by when he was in Nashville recording an album. He loved my country ham breakfasts.

One time Billy Bob Thornton and Angelina Jolie stopped by the house. They were driving an old Winnebago to California, where they would get married. Marty was over recording with John, and I fixed everybody a big breakfast.

After we ate, Billy Bob asked, "Anybody smoke?" June forbade smoking in the house, so he took a group of people out in the yard to smoke.

Billy Graham was a special friend for more than thirty years. He first sought John out in 1970. At the time, Billy was feeling alienated from his son Franklin, and he thought John was "cool" enough to help him bridge the generation gap.

Billy and his wife Ruth came to visit many times, in Hendersonville, in Florida, and in Jamaica. John and June went up to Charlotte, North Carolina, to visit them at their home.

Billy loved to go deep-sea fishing with John. One day they brought back a huge catch of shrimp, and Ruth helped me and Maybelle cook them for dinner.

Whenever they'd visit, Ruth would be the first one up and make coffee for everybody. The four of them—Ruth, Billy, June, and John—would hang around the house talking about the Bible, religion, and problems with their kids.

The Grahams attended John's concerts whenever they were in the area, and John and June often sang at the Billy Graham Crusades.

At one of the Crusades June said it was so hot up on

Billy Graham sought John out to help Billy relate to his son.

the platform that they had ice in plastic bags around their feet trying to keep cool. June said: "Billy, hell ain't half a mile away."

When Dr. Graham was in the Mayo Clinic in Minnesota, June, John, and I flew up to see about him. A nurse drove him to a nearby park to meet us, and June and John talked with him while they walked through the park. After that, Billy, John, and June all were getting sick and couldn't visit anymore.

Fans

THROUGHOUT THEIR CAREERS John and June always made time for their fans. Even when they were dog-tired after a show, they'd still sign autographs or stop and talk for a minute if they had the time.

John would sign autographs until every last fan had one. One time a couple drove up in a beautiful new Mercedes. They handed John a marker and had him autograph the trunk! "Now I've signed everything," John laughed.

A lot of fans would come running up and say, "Hi, Johnny Cash." Then they'd look at June and say, "Hi, Loretta!" It didn't bother her, though. All she'd say is, "Honey, I'm not Loretta. I'm June Carter Cash."

I wasn't around the music business long before I figured out that for every nice fan there was a crazy one. We saw plenty of both kinds, especially on the road.

Over the years we saw some fans so often, they became our friends. My friend Dennis Devine is proba-

Dennis Devine was one of John's favorite fans.

bly John's Number One fan of all time. Dennis first met
John when Dennis was just a kid, back in February 1960
at a concert in Omaha. John took him backstage and they
became friends.

He followed John ever since then, attending as many
concerts as he could all over the country. I think he's got a
ticket stub from every show that John ever performed. He's
also got about every album John ever put out, and all kinds
of Cash memorabilia.

It's easy to get caught up in Dennis's excitement. One
time he learned that the tour would be in his home state,
Iowa, on John's birthday in 1987. The next thing we knew,
Dennis had arranged a birthday party for John—at the governor's mansion! Governor Terry Brandstad made John an
honorary citizen of the state of Iowa.

Dennis has his headstone all ready for when he passes away. It has his picture and John's picture engraved side by side.

Barbara Sather from Wisconsin is another longtime fan I've come to love. She and her husband Bill went to as many concerts as she could. John once said that Barbara was always faithful to him.

She and Bill always sent special gifts at Christmas time, and they would send us flowers and candy when we were on the road.

Barbara was kind and thoughtful–she tried not to bother John and June. She loved to go backstage, but she wouldn't go until she was invited. She always said John and June needed their privacy, and she wasn't going to impose.

Dennis Devine once set up a birthday party for John at Iowa governor Terry Branstad's house.

June visits with Louise Klein and Barbara Sather at a fan club event.

She was one of the most active members of the official Johnny Cash fan club—she was involved for more than twenty-five years.

At its height, the fan club probably had ten thousand members. Curtis and Alma Todd and Jeannie and Ray Witherell ran it. They wrote letters asking people to join and sent out a newsletter called the "Fan Club Book," with concert schedules and pictures from recent shows.

If they were in town, John and June hosted a fan club breakfast every year on the day after Fan Fair closed in Nashville, usually at a Shoney's restaurant. The breakfast gave people a chance to meet their idols. The fans would give them gifts like books, framed photos, and handmade ceramics and afghans. John and June saved all of that stuff.

One year the whole fan club made Christmas ornaments for John and June. They received hundreds and put every single one of them on their tree.

Fans came from all over the world to see John and June perform. Every year four or five fans from Germany would save up their money and come to the United States to follow the tour for three or four weeks.

Sometimes you just couldn't get away from the fans—especially on the road. We made hotel reservations under another name, but every time we hit the lobby it was full of fans. John and June were always gracious about it.

One time we were getting on the elevator at the hotel when we heard a woman yelling "Johnny Cash!" John turned around to talk to her and the door closed right on his head. We were poking at the buttons trying to get the door back open, and John just stood talking to her with the door squeezing his face.

June said, "Oh, John, you're going to cut your head off!" He and the fan kept talking until we got his head out and the door closed.

John was always bringing special fans backstage when we were touring. He played "Orange Blossom Special" with two harmonicas, and every night he'd give them to somebody in the audience, especially young kids. I'd stand offstage and he'd bring them to me, telling me who he'd picked out. "Give these to that little girl in the wheelchair," he'd say. Many times he'd tell me to bring some of them

Fans knew June loved flowers and brought or sent bouquets.

backstage after the show to meet him. It was always the thrill of their lives.

After the show there'd be more autographs to sign. And then we still weren't through with the fans. When the bus pulled out after a show, people would start chasing after us, staying right on our bumper. The bus driver, J.P. Powell, was really good at shaking them off.

One time Helen, Anita, and her daughter Lorrie left a fan a little shook up. They were leaving a festival, and fans were swarming around their van. They took off driving across a field with a guy chasing them on a bicycle.

June was always glad to sign autographs.

"I'll take care of him," Lorrie said. She opened the van door and the man ran smack into it. They weren't going very fast so nobody was hurt.

In all the time I knew him, there was just one time that John Cash wouldn't sign an autograph. John and June's good friend Chet Atkins died in 2001. I drove them to the visitation at Roesch-Patton funeral home in Nashville, where I let them out and went to park the car.

When I got back, John said, "Let's go" and we left. People had been bugging him for autographs there at the funeral home. "I couldn't even pay my respects," John said.

And then as we were leaving, even the policemen asked for an autograph. John was real upset about it.

Sometimes the fans were, well, just confused. I was up at the House of Cash when a tour bus pulled in. The One-Piece-at-a-Time Car was in the parking lot. Well, this woman was just sure that John himself had built the car—by stealing the parts from the factory. I heard her saying, "I worked at the factory in Detroit where he took the parts one at a time to build the car." She must have been confusing his song with reality.

I don't know how the story got started, but many fans "knew for a fact" that John had been in prison. They were always asking me, "Now just how long was he in for?" The truth is, John never went to prison except to perform. (He did go to jail a few times, including once for picking flowers out of a woman's yard in Mississippi.)

It was also "common knowledge" that the big scar on John's face was from a gunshot wound. Really, it was just where he'd had a cyst removed one time.

Some fans loved John and June a little too much. One woman always gave John a big old slobbery kiss on the lips whenever she saw him. "You're gonna have to stop kissing me 'cause I might get AIDS," he told her.

Well, the next time we saw her, she marched up and gave him another big kiss. "You don't have to worry about me giving you AIDS, and here's the proof." She'd gone out and had herself tested for AIDS and brought him the results!

One German fan went way too far. June saw her outside the show with a bloody arm. Being June, she just had to try to help. The girl pulled off the bandage and showed how she'd carved "JRC" and "JCC" in her arm with a razor blade!

June was horrified, and then she got mad. "I never want to see you at our show again if you do this."

We did see her again on next tour and she showed us her scars.

I ran into one fan at June's funeral who was more than a little confused. We got to talking and she told me she'd been taking care of June for the last five years. "You did, huh?" was all I said. I'd never seen her before in my life! I just let her talk, and I never let on that it was really me who had been taking care of June.

"Every Road in This Here Land"

JOHN AND JUNE took me to every state but Alaska. Besides that, we traveled to Canada, England, Ireland, and Wales; France, Germany and Austria; Belgium and Holland; Norway, Denmark, and Finland; Sweden and Switzerland; Poland and Czechoslovakia; Israel, and Australia and New Zealand.

When John sang "I've been everywhere, man" he really meant it.

We put a lot of miles on the tour bus and sat in more airports than I cared to see. But I enjoyed life on the road. There was always something to do on the bus. I liked waking up in a different city every morning. And we had a lot of fun.

When we flew, we usually took a private jet. We'd leave out of the Gallatin airport. It had short little runways that scared you to death thinking you weren't going to get off the ground before the runway ran out.

June really hated to fly out of Gallatin. But she was scared of flying anyway. As many airplanes as she went on, she was afraid to fly all her life.

If we could get someplace driving, we'd take the bus. It was mostly just for traveling—we tried to stay in a nice hotel nearly everywhere we went. The bus had plenty of room for everybody, though. When June's sisters Helen and Anita traveled with us, their room was at the very back. It had two couches that made into beds.

The next room was June's bedroom. Then came the bathroom and kitchen. I cooked many a meal there.

John's bedroom was next, and there were two more couches up behind the driver. I didn't sleep much on the

We put in a lot of miles on the tour bus.

bus, but I could pull a curtain around one of these couches if I wanted to lie down. June had a big chair in her room that would lay back, and I'd doze off in it. Or if Anita and Helen weren't with us, I'd use their room.

Before heading out on a tour, I'd make sure the bus was clean, put fresh linens on the beds, stock the refrigerator, and buy supplies. Then we'd pack the clothes.

The bus had a couple of closets where we hung John's and June's stage clothes. John usually packed his own clothes; he was very neat. June always took three times as much as she needed. I had to make sure we had all of her shoes that matched her stage outfits.

Before every trip, we stopped at the video store to get movies, movies, movies, and buy some more at Wal-Mart.

I stayed busy as we rolled along, cleaning up and taking care of everybody. I'd vacuum and dust and clean the bathroom. I kept the drink box filled and bought groceries for the good-sized refrigerator.

I cooked when we got tired of road food. I'd make chicken and dumplings, green beans, pinto beans—anything that was good slow-cooked.

One time I was making quesadillas for lunch. I was about ready to turn them over when June said, "Honey, let me show you how to flip them." She showed me, all right— the quesadilla ended up on the floor.

"Oh, June, now I'll have to fix another one," I said.

She scooped it up and put it back in the skillet. "Don't worry about that; we'll just give it to Helen," she said. And she did.

Helen was a lot of fun while traveling.

We didn't tell Helen until she'd finished eating. She wasn't real happy, but June told her, "It's fine. The skillet was so hot it killed all the germs."

There was often a card game or dominoes or Scrabble going on. We were playing Scrabble with Helen one time and she accidentally spelled a dirty word. John started teasing her right off: "Helen, you've done gone talking nasty," he said. June gave her a look and acted like she was serious. "Honey, we don't talk ugly on this bus," she said.

June didn't care much for games, though. She'd take her sewing basket with her and crochet little caps in all sizes. Mostly, however, she'd lie in bed and read mysteries and Stephen King books for the whole trip, whether it was one hour or ten hours.

Helen read all the time, too. She loved every kind of book.

Helen was really a trip—it was a lot of fun to be on the road with her. She was always getting mixed up. Every time she said "I don't want to hear that" she'd cover up her eyes. If she said, "That's something I don't want to see" she'd put her hands over her ears.

We would play practical jokes on Helen because she was the kind of person you could do that to. She was just so gullible. You could tell that girl anything and likely as not she'd believe it.

Many times she'd come back to a completely empty hotel room: The band, the sound crew, and I would move every stick of furniture into the room next door. She'd be

John Carter joins June on stage for a song. That's a young Marty Stuart behind him.

on the phone saying, "I know y'all did this. Give me back my furniture."

After a show we'd run through the halls picking up everybody's room service trays. We'd make a tower of them leaning against Helen's door. She'd open it up and the huge pile of dishes would crash into her room. She was always a good sport about it.

Helen could get in bed faster than anybody. By the time the rest of us got to the hotel after a show, Helen would already be running up and down the hall in her nightgown. John called it a helen. He'd say, "Well here comes Helen in her helen." One night he was wearing pajamas and said he had on his helens.

We ran into Helen out in the hotel hallway one time. She was standing in front of a shoeshine machine with an ice bucket wondering where the ice came out. From then on, every time somebody saw a shoeshine machine they'd ask Helen if she needed any ice.

Once in England the whole lot of us piled onto one of those double-decker buses. The top was full and she was downstairs with the band. Now the driver sits on the top level, but Helen didn't know that. All she knew was that there wasn't anybody at the front of the bus.

The band starting joking around. "If that driver don't hurry up, I'm going to drive this bus myself," one said.

Helen was telling them, "Now don't do that. You'll get us all in trouble."

About that time the bus driver upstairs started up, and Helen took off down the aisle yelling. She just knew that one of the band members was driving.

One time Helen had a real scare on the road, but everything turned out all right. Loretta Lynn and Conway Twitty were touring up in Nova Scotia when Loretta got sick. Three days before the show, the promoters called John and asked him if he could fill in. He said he could, and invited Helen and Anita to go with him.

June and John were going to fly in the day of the show, while the rest of us loaded up the tour bus and hit the road with two drivers. One slept while the other one drove. Nova Scotia is a real long way–it took us fifty-four hours to drive it!

About halfway there we stopped at a truck stop. Helen

On the road in 1977 are Helen, Jan Howard, Anita, June, and John.

went to get off the bus and slipped on some diesel fuel. She fell flat on her face. The truck stop manager came running out and we picked Helen up and got her back on the bus.

She tried to say she was okay, but the manager called an ambulance so they could check her over.

The stretcher wouldn't fit on the bus, so Helen walked to the door. We teased her because she had to walk so they could put her on a stretcher. Outside they rolled up behind her and stood the stretcher on end. She was the funniest-looking thing, standing straight up strapped to the stretcher.

She had a couple of bruises on her head and her hands were skinned up, but otherwise she was okay. But it took four or five hours at the hospital for them to check her out. We hit the road hard after that and rolled into Nova Scotia just in time for the show.

Helen and I made a nightmare trip to Branson that I'll never forget. I picked her up at her house in Dickson, loading her guitar and three big suitcases in the Lincoln Town Car (black, of course) that John had rented. We were ten miles the other side of Paducah, Kentucky, when I hit something. I stomped on the brakes and stopped in the middle of I-24. The airbags had gone off and nearly killed us both. Helen was riding with her feet up on the dash, and I don't know how the airbag didn't snap her in half.

I ran around to Helen's side to get her out. She was trying to touch her nose with her finger, wailing, "My nose is gone, my nose is gone!"

"No, it's not," I told her. "It's on your face." That settled her down and I started looking for help. A semi-truck blew by without stopping even though we were in the middle of the road. I flagged a car down and got a guy and his buddy to help us.

When they pushed the car back to get it out of the road, out popped a big old deer from under the car. When I hit him he'd gone up on the hood, and when I hit the brakes he slid off and under the car. There was blood everywhere.

Before I got in the ambulance I told the police we were on the way to Branson with a carful of luggage. They were really kind. The police took our stuff, waited for us at the hospital while we got checked out, and then drove us to a little motel down the street. It was three a.m. by this time.

The manager found us a room, but it only had one bed. I'd tried sleeping with Helen in the past, and I just wouldn't do it again. She'd read a while, turn the light off, and lie there for a while. Then she'd say, "I can't sleep," turn the light on, and wake everybody up. She was always up and down like a yoyo all night long.

The manager found us another room with two beds. I was exhausted, couldn't wait to lie down. I pulled the covers back and somebody had made the bed up with dirty sheets. So we got a third room.

By now it was four-thirty in the morning. I called our hotel in Branson and told them we'd had a wreck. They offered to send a car, but the road manager had already arranged for a car to be available at noon. But it was three hours late. We finally rolled into Branson about nine at night. That was one long trip.

Foreign tours were always exhausting. We really had to push hard. We flew when we had to and rode the double-decker bus if we didn't.

That bus wasn't near as nice as ours back home. And bumpy! You could hardly stay in your seat. We didn't have our own rooms on the bus, just an aisle with bunk beds on either side. John always took the bottom, June got the middle, and I slept in the top bunk.

On free days, I'd go sightseeing with John and June. We visited a lot of old churches all over Europe. They shopped every where we went, buying furniture and other antiques.

On show days I kept busy taking care of John and June: getting them—and all their stuff—off the bus and into the dressing room. They'd take a nap before the concert and I'd get set up to sell souvenirs, counting everything and getting a list of foreign money so I'd know how to make change.

I sold everything: hats, bandanas, key chains, photos, books, even a nightgown that said, "I'm sleeping with Johnny Cash."

On a German tour Anita and I made us a little extra pocket money. The Elvis stamps had just come out and we took a bunch of rolls with us. Of course, the Germans couldn't get those and went nuts for them. We sold them for twenty-five dollars a stamp.

I'd sell souvenirs until after the show, then we'd load them on the bus with the instruments and head for the next stop.

I met one of my dearest friends on the road in Paris. When we stayed in hotels, John and June nearly always had room service. I liked to get out so I'd go down to the hotel restaurant.

One time while I was eating, "Jackson" started playing on the restaurant's loudspeakers. I overheard a woman at the table next to me saying that Johnny Cash was her parents' favorite singer. They had tickets to the show that night.

Well, she talked kind of funny so I stopped by her table on the way out and asked them, "What planet are y'all from?"

Turns out the woman was best-selling novelist Linda Miller from Seattle. Naturally, they thought I talked funny, too, and wanted to know what I was doing so far away from home. You should have seen the looks on their faces when I said I worked for Johnny Cash!

The next day we were checking out of the hotel and Linda was there in the lobby. I introduced her to John and told him what she'd said about her parents. When he found out they were heading for London same as us, he got them box seats for the show at the Royal Albert Hall.

When I got to my hotel there in London I found a package as big as a hatbox full of chocolates from Harrods, the famous department store. They were from Linda. I've never seen so many different kinds of chocolate in my life. I shared them with John, who really loved chocolate.

June got a huge bouquet of flowers from Linda. She always loved flowers so much, but she kept eyeing John's share of the chocolates. Finally she broke down and said real pitiful, "I'll trade you some flowers for chocolates." He just laughed and gave her some.

Linda helped me out in the restaurant there at the hotel. I was having a sandwich and picked up a little square box on the table. I kept fiddling with it, turning it this way and that, while I waited for my order.

Meanwhile my waiter was coming around every couple of minutes, it seemed like. "Madam, may I help you?" he kept asking. I'd tell him no, I was fine, but a few minutes later here he came again. He was awful attentive; I thought maybe he was sucking up for a big tip or something.

That night I met Linda in the restaurant for dinner.

I walked in and there was that same waiter. He had such a funny look on his face, like "Oh no, here she comes again!"

Linda and I sat down and there was another one of those boxes. I was telling her about lunch while I fiddled with it some more. Here came that waiter again. Linda looked at him, and at me, and at that little box, and just busted out laughing. Finally she let me in on the joke: It was a call box, and I'd been ringing for the waiter every time I played with it!

Linda and I have been friends ever since, and we still laugh about that little box. She even dedicated one of her books to me. It says, "Don't stop talking to strangers," in honor of how we met.

I only saw Elvis once, and that was in Las Vegas. He finished his show and came down to John and June's dressing room. Maybelle was the only one there, and she talked to him in the doorway for a while. He must have had fifteen or twenty security guards with him. They completely filled up the hallway.

Another time when John was playing Vegas, I messed up my knee something terrible. The casino staff always tried to get up a softball game against any touring groups staying at the hotel. The band, along with Helen, Anita, and me, were playing one time and the ball got away from Hugh Waddell (John's publicist at the time) and banged into my knee. I kept getting fluid building up, and for months I had to have it drained ever so often.

We put together a softball team to play against the casino workers.

One day it was so swollen I could hardly walk. A friend of Anita's came to visit and offered to drain it on the spot. It turned out he was a mortician. I figured he could work on live people as well as dead people, so he grabbed a needle and drained it right then and there.

I finally had to have surgery on my leg–the doctor got in there and scraped down my shinbone. I was in a cast of one kind or another for nearly a year, but about three weeks after the operation John called me. "We miss you on the road," he said. "It's time for you to get back to touring."

That's just part of the job: The show must go on.

* * *

We always had a lot of fun when John played the casinos. We hit them all: Vegas, Lake Tahoe, Sam's Town in Tunica, and even Foxwood up in Connecticut. After the show he'd give us each a hundred dollars and we'd all go gamble.

Well, except for June. She wasn't big on gambling. She used to say if she ever won the lottery she would give me and the other girls who worked there a million dollars. John used to tease her about it. He'd say, "Babe, how are you ever going to win if you don't ever play?"

Anyway, the rest of us would hit the casino. John also gave us money to play roulette for him. We'd put ten dollars each on 2, 4, 6, 8, and 10. He probably won more than he lost that way. We'd take him his winnings, but by the end of the night he had usually given it all back to us.

I think Maybelle had as much fun as anybody. I remember one night after a show in Vegas she said to me, "Let's go change our clothes and come back down to the casino."

Maybelle loved the slots—that was about all she would play. She yanked on those levers until two a.m. or so and told me, "I'm gonna go back upstairs. I need to lie down."

I got her settled in her room and went back to the casino. Blackjack's my game. I played for a couple of hours and got to talking to a big chicken farmer from Louisiana.

Around four a.m. I looked up and here came Maybelle. She'd had a rest and was ready for more action! I guess we played until seven in the morning before we

Maybelle loved to play her autoharp.

called it a night—or called it a day, I guess. We slept a little while and then got up for a big breakfast.

Maybelle sure was a trouper. She toured with John and June until the late Seventies, just a couple of years before she died. John would call her out on stage and she'd sing a song or two; later on she wasn't up to singing and only took a bow. Everywhere we went the crowd just loved her. Helen and Anita were chips off her block. Anita finally had to give up the road—she had rheumatoid arthritis and could hardly walk across the floor. Helen sang with John and June until they stopped touring. She passed away in 1998, and Anita died in 1999.

Like I said, we tried to stay in hotels anytime we could. John and June always got a suite or at least two rooms with a door between them. There were a couple of reasons for that: John always liked to take a nap up in the day but June never did. And neither one of them wanted to share a bathroom with the other.

Well, one time they had rooms side by side but there wasn't a connecting door. John took care of that. He just bashed a big hole in the wall!

Anytime we were near Pennsylvania, the Hershey factory would send John a bunch of five-pound Hershey Bars. They were big old suckers, nearly two feet long.

One day John broke off a hunk and went to take his nap. After a while I heard June screeching from his room.

"Wake up, honey," she said. "John, what's wrong with you?"

I got in there and boy, did he look awful. Then we figured out what it was and started laughing.

He'd fallen asleep with that candy in his hand. He always flopped around a lot in his sleep, and the chocolate had melted all over him. It was on his face, in his hair, all over his clothes, just everywhere. We had to strip the bed because there was chocolate all over the sheets and covers.

Finally, life on the road got to be too much for John and June. One night John looked out at the audience and told a band member, "We better get off the road. There's nobody but blue heads and white heads coming to see us."

But it was John's health that decided matters. In 1997, we were in New York for an appearance on "Good Morning America" to promote John's book *Cash*. Back at the hotel, June called me. "Come up here quick. John's fallen in the bathroom and I need help." When we finally got him up, he said, "I'm just too weak to be out on the road working. We're going home tomorrow."

He made a few appearances here and there, but he never toured again.

Homes Away
From Home

JOHN AND JUNE were always itching to go somewhere. Sometimes it seemed like they were never happy
at home. I think it's because people there were constantly
wanting something from them.

We'd go to the Four Seasons in Beverly Hills for a
while, then head for the Plaza Athenée in New York for
some shopping or off to Canada for a vacation.

Sometimes we'd just need to get away from it all. After
a long tour or a spell of cold weather or when we were
tired of the city, we'd head for the beach.

Maybelle and Eck had a real nice house in New Port
Richey, Florida, on the Gulf coast just north of Tampa.
Eck's twin sister Virgie lived in the town, and he and May-
belle bought the house to be close to her.

When Maybelle died, Helen and Anita sold their
share to John and June. That house was in the family for
more than fifty years.

We had plenty of room for ourselves and guests: The

The Florida house was in the family for more than fifty years.

house has six bedrooms and five baths plus the living room, dining room, and kitchen.

It didn't look like much from the outside, but we did what we could to spruce it up. I bet I painted that house three or four times while I was with Maybelle.

I remember one time Maybelle's brother Toob and I were getting ready to put another coat of paint on the house. While I wasn't looking, he turned the pressure washer on me and nearly blew my bathing suit off! He laughed about that for a long time.

We had to get some emergency repairs done one time. John had been there for a while before June and I arrived. I carried my clothes to my bedroom and saw that water had been leaking in. I looked closer and saw that the ceiling tiles were full of holes.

I called June to take a look. "I don't know what John's done now," she said and went looking for him.

"Honey, what in the world happened to the ceiling in Peggy's bedroom?" she asked John.

"Oh, I went back there and laid down, and I just wanted to shoot my gun," he said kind of sheepishly. "I was just having fun."

"I can't believe you did that," June said. She told me later she kind of got on John about that.

I always looked forward to going down there. Maybelle and I spent hours sitting on the dock fishing and talking. We'd go to the dog races and the horse races. We'd run into baseball stars Pete Rose and Joe Torre, sharing the box seats of one of Maybelle's friends.

We went deep sea fishing all the time. I never got seasick but once, but that was a doozy. I was okay until I went to drop my line. I guess it was looking at the water that did it, but I was the sickest I've ever been in my whole life. I finally crawled up on the motor housing and fell asleep.

When I woke up, there was Maybelle asleep beside me. She'd gotten seasick, too.

John was real big on fishing. He had a big map up on the wall where he kept track of all our fishing trips. He'd mark when we went out, who was there, how far we went, and what we caught.

We were out about thirty miles one day and fished until it started to get dark. The motor wouldn't start.

June was just sure we were going to be stranded out there and lost at sea.

No problem, John said; there's a second motor under the deck. Well, he couldn't lift very much so it was up to me to get the motor up. Then John held onto it while I got in the water. Of course, I can't swim a lick. But I had to try, so I put on a lifejacket and somehow we got the motor in place without sinking to the bottom. I climbed back in and hooked up the gas line. We like to never have got that thing started but finally made it home. I added "boat repair" to my resumé that day.

John and June loved seafood and would have eaten it every night if you gave it to them. I used to get up at four in the morning and wait for the shrimp boats to come in. When I saw their lights in the harbor, I'd grab a bucket and head on over. They'd give me a bucketful of the biggest shrimp you've ever seen.

New Port Richey is a pretty small town, so we'd go over to Tarpon Springs to eat seafood.

One time we were eating with a doctor friend of theirs and his secretary, and suddenly the doctor's head fell right in his plate.

"John, the doctor's sick," June said.

"No, June, the doctor's drunk," said John.

We got him upright, but a little while later it happened again. We thought we better pour him in his car and get him home.

The four of us got him out to the lobby. "I'll go get the car. It's parked down the street," said the secretary. She took off out the door and she never came back. We finally managed to get him home ourselves.

Besides seafood, fruit was always on the menu in Florida. We had as much fruit as we could eat: The yard had orange, lemon, and grapefruit trees. The oranges and lemons were huge, as big as the grapefruits. If nobody was staying there when they ripened, John and June would send somebody down in a truck to pick fruit and bring it back to Hendersonville.

Florida was great, but when we were dead tired from being on the road, we'd head for Jamaica. John and June loved it so. In the early years we'd leave right after Christmas and stay until spring when Jamaica started getting too hot. By the end we were staying there probably three or four months out of the year, heading down before Thanksgiving.

John and June's home in Jamaica is called the Cinnamon Hill Great House, and now it's a Jamaican National Monument. It was built in 1747 on a huge sugar plantation by the Barrett family. Poet Elizabeth Barrett Browning's father was born there.

John bought the house and about fifteen acres from his good friend John Rollins, who had developed the property, restored several eighteenth-century mansions, and built a resort including the Cinnamon Hill and White Witch golf

The Jamaica house had a beautiful waterfall nearby.

courses. Rollins and his wife Michelle lived nearby in Rose Hall Great House.

Cinnamon Hill was absolutely beautiful, a real tropical paradise. Big bushes full of flowers grew wild in the yard. The beach was sparkling white next to the deep blue water. There was a beautiful waterfall beside the golf course, where the native women would come there, strip down naked, and take a bath.

We had all the fruit we could eat growing right there on the property: mangoes, papayas, oranges, bananas, and breadfruit. You don't know what bananas taste like until you've pulled one off a tree. Aloe vera plants as big around as foot tubs grew everywhere; the Jamaicans used the plant for medicine, eating the gel inside and rubbing it on burns.

The house has long porches on both sides, one looking out over the golf course and the other facing the ocean, where you could catch the breeze off the water. We spent a lot of time relaxing on those porches.

You entered the huge living room through either porch. The big dining room had a table that seated twenty-four people. The small dining room was cozier. We had lunch there, and John and I would go there to play dominoes.

The long hallway leading to the kitchen was big enough to be a sitting room with sofas and chairs. The first floor had three bedrooms. John called one of them the Billy Graham Room. That's where frequent visitors Billy and Ruth Graham always stayed when they came to visit. They used a second big bedroom with a king-size bed to watch television, during the day and some at night. Upstairs, June had claimed the bathroom in the master bedroom. John and I each had a bath off the hall. My bedroom was next to the master suite. I could lie in bed and see the sky–day or night–through the roof shingles. When it rained the shingles would swell up, and the roof wouldn't leak no matter how hard it rained.

June was scared silly of storms. Off the first floor was a concrete storm cellar complete with shower and bath. If there was a threat of a big storm, June would say, "Y'all come on, let's go to the storm room." We'd troop in there and wait it out. The storms never lasted very long. After a bit John would get antsy. "Come on, let's get out of here," he'd say. But June always wanted us to stay a little longer.

The house had a big staff so I didn't have many of my usual duties–it was always kind of a vacation for me, too. Desna, her daughter Donna, and her son Carl handled most of the house work. Carl was a minister and took Sundays off to tend to his congregation.

Geraldine did the laundry and ironing. Pansy was the seamstress who made clothes and household things for June. Melvin was the yardman. He lived on the grounds and kept chickens, goats, and a horse. He'd sell us fresh eggs for breakfast.

I only cooked when John and June wanted something the Jamaicans didn't know how to make. I'd smuggle country ham in my suitcase so we could have our regular breakfast. I slid packages of Harper's Country ham in between

Going to Jamaica was partly a vacation for me, too.

all my clothes. I couldn't get buttermilk for my biscuits, so I soured milk with vinegar.

On a typical day, John would be up by three or four a.m. He'd peck on my door and say, "Peggy, time to get up" or make enough racket to rouse me. I'd make us some coffee and he'd say, "Let's play some dominoes." We'd play until Desna and Donna got there to make breakfast. We'd have fruit punch on one of the porches, and they'd serve us breakfast there or by the swimming pool.

Carl set a beautiful table. June, of course, made sure we used linen tablecloths and napkins, china, crystal, and silver, even out by the swimming pool.

After breakfast we'd ride golf carts through the course to a place by the sea where June would lead us in prayers. John and June called it their Inspiration Point.

We'd ride around the golf course, usually with John and June singing up a storm. One time John was driving down a little hill and hit the brakes because he thought he was going too fast. It had been raining and they hit a wet spot. I was driving along behind them and all of a sudden that golf cart started spinning around and around, with John trying to get it under control and June hollering her head off. They finally hit some grass that stopped them, but it was a close call.

John would sit on the porch and whittle. He'd get some sticks and carve crosses and hearts that he hung on the trees. Once he even whittled a walking stick.

Sometimes we'd visit with John and Michelle Rollins. We'd have lunch and play bingo and other games. Lots of times their four teenaged children would come over for breakfast.

John usually took a little nap before lunch while June read or watched the big-screen TV. The satellite dish had

June always wore a hat outside in Jamaica because she was sensitive to the sun.

more than nine hundred channels, so there was always something to see.

After lunch John would take a big nap, from about one to four p.m. June would nap, or she and I would often go shopping. We had to take Carl along to hang onto our purses. Otherwise a group of Jamaicans would surround us, and while one of them talked to us the others would try to grab our stuff.

I'd always bring John back that day's *New York Times* and *USA Today*, which didn't arrive until the afternoon.

If they were both napping I'd go down to the beach with a metal detector. I found all kinds of stuff: gold rings, silver necklaces, and two hundred sixty-five dollars in nickels, dimes, quarters, and half dollars.

Other days I stayed busy weed-eating, chopping down bushes, or tending my tomato plants. Usually, I only had two or three, but that kept us in tomatoes the whole time we were there.

I could always wander around the yard picking up golf balls people had hit out of bounds. One time I gathered up two hundred and gave them to my brother-in-law Wayne.

About five-thirty we'd have dinner by candlelight in the big dining room and have our dessert in the drawing room.

June loved cheesecake, so that was often what we had. I'd go down to the Wyndham Rose Hall Resort and buy one or two nearly every day. Finally the manager couldn't stand it anymore. "What are you doing with all those cheesecakes! You're not selling them, are you?" I laughed and told him what a big fan the cheesecakes had.

Some evenings we'd ride through the golf course after everybody was finished playing. Or there were always movies to watch. The ones you could rent locally were bad copies, so the office would send us tapes in the mail. John and June liked westerns, Clint Eastwood movies, and Bobby Duvall's movies.

Many nights John would say, "Peggy, let's go play dominoes." We'd always ask June to join us, but she usually said, "I think I'll just paddle on upstairs."

We'd play until he went to bed, usually about eight. I never went to bed until they did.

Every so often the kids would come down and stay for a few days. Some of June's family would visit, too. Her cousin Esther and husband Burl Moore came down several times, and I'd drive them around. Burl and I had a running

For Christmas in Jamaica, we'd decorate with pine branches.

joke: I'd ask him where he'd parked my car, and he'd say, "It's always your car when you want to drive, but my car when it's out of gas."

We got to where we were spending Christmas in Jamaica every year at the end. One or another of the kids might bring the family down, but sometimes it was just me, John, and June.

We'd make our own Christmas tree. The natives would climb the pine trees and cut off branches. June would put them in a big clay pot and decorate with lights and red bows. We three would exchange presents; they'd send their gifts to the children and grandchildren.

One of my happiest memories from Jamaica was June's daughter Rosey's wedding to Phillip Adams in 2002. The staff and I went down to the local hardware store and gathered up metal tubing, some wire, and paint. We built an arch and painted everything white, then decorated it with flowers from the yard.

I helped build and decorate this arch for Rosey's wedding.

I helped Rosey get dressed, and she was really glowing that day. The decorated arch made it a beautiful ceremony.

That same year we held John's last birthday party for just a few friends and the staff. We didn't have any decorations, so we got these long, fuzzy flowers from the yard and spelled out, "Happy 70th Birthday, Johnny Cash."

Somebody dug up some Jamaican tam caps with long, curly dreadlocks attached. John was a good sport about

John put on his dreadlocks for his birthday.

wearing his. June, of course, was always willing to try a new hat. John played host, serving cake—white with white Splenda icing made by the Wyndham Hotel baker.

John would spend his next—and last—birthday in the hospital.

Sick and Tired

JOHN AND JUNE were both getting old and tired. Starting in 2001, they were in the hospital nearly twenty different times. In a couple of years, June logged forty-five days in the hospital diagnosed with pneumonia, leaking heart valves, congestive heart failure, and gallstones. On her last trip to the hospital I stayed there with June eighteen straight days until the hearse came for her body.

John had lived hard for a lot of years, and his body was just plain wearing out. He spent a total of a hundred twenty-five days in the hospital from 2001 until June's death. He had a medical book full of problems: Shy-Drager Syndrome, eye problems, diabetes, foot problems, fluid retention, kidney failure, staph infections, injuries from several falls, a toe amputation, a sedative overdose, a foot ulcer, ankle problems, bleeding problems, and several cases of pneumonia.

I feel like for the last ten years, I spent half my life at Baptist Hospital in Nashville. The doctors and nurses all knew me by name. It got so I'd take John home from the hospital and tell the staff, "I'll be back soon with June."

We went so much it became a routine. It was really like moving, or going on tour.

To protect their privacy, John and June checked into the hospital under fake names. John usually used the name "Malcolm Kilgore," a relative's name. June used her favorite cousin's name, "Fern Salyers."

We always had the same suite on the eighth floor at Baptist. I don't know if they just kept it open for John and June or kicked people out when we showed up, but it was always available when we needed it. The suite had a sitting room with a dining table and chairs and a microwave. John had a room on one side and June had a room on the other. The couch in the sitting room turned into a bed, so I stayed there where I could hear them both.

Even in the hospital, June insisted on making a home. We brought in our own table linens and napkins, crystal, china, and silver. My sister Betty would bring food and clean linens to the hospital every day and take the dirty ones home to wash.

June also brought her own down comforters and pillows—she would have used her own sheets on the bed but the hospital wouldn't let her.

I made many a food run to Elliston Place down the street from the hospital. I'd go to a Japanese place to get sushi for June. John didn't care for that, so I'd go to Elliston Place Soda Shop to get him a vegetable plate.

John and June were both pretty good patients, but

John would get testy sometimes. He could be grumpy when he didn't feel good. If we didn't bring his coffee fast enough, that coffee cup would go flying across the room!

One time he was trying to tell the nurse something or other and accused her of not listening to him. She told him, "No, sir, I'm just like you. I can't hear anything." He'd slide down in the bed and it would take two or three of us to pull him back up. "I know y'all don't like me," he'd complain, "but don't kill me!"

We always had a parade of visitors coming through the hospital. Family came by to tell John they loved him: his sisters Louise, Reba, and Joanne visited with his brother Tommy. The girls were in and out, especially Kathy, Cindy and Rosanne, who was there a lot. John Carter didn't come around very much.

Music friends like Waylon Jennings (before he died) and his wife Jessi Colter, and Marty Stuart and his wife Connie Smith would drop in. Other friends like Jane Seymour and her husband James Keach visited several times.

Even among all the sickness there was some joy. When John was in the hospital for open-heart surgery, one of his friends brought his fiancée by to visit. They knew John was an ordained minister—he'd performed the wedding ceremonies for A.P.'s son Joe Carter and for his daughter Kathy—and mentioned they'd like John to marry them.

"Okay," John said, "but it will have to be right now."

Believe it or not, they agreed. The president of the hospital, David Stringfield, had dropped in to visit. John told him he was the best man. "I'll stand up with you," June said. I ran down to the gift shop and bought flowers for the bride's bouquet. We had a real sweet wedding right there in John's hospital room.

I've always been pretty healthy, but one time while John was in the hospital I had a real scare. I woke up and didn't know where I was. It was like I was floating out of my body. I was afraid I was having a heart attack or a stroke.

Somehow I got up and pulled open the heavy door. I fell right out in the hallway and couldn't move.

The nurses' station was right down the hall and they saw me lying there. "What's wrong with Peggy?" I heard someone say.

They told me later I'd done turned gray. It was really lucky I was at the hospital when this happened. I think if I'd been at home I would have died before anybody could help me.

They rushed me to the ER. Soon I had IVs in both arms and an oxygen mask on my face. My blood pressure was 50/30. (Normal is 120/80, so I was running pretty low.)

"Do you want me to wake John up?" the nurse asked. "No, he needs his rest. Let him sleep," I said. She asked me if I wanted her to call Betty.

"Not unless I get worse," I told her.

She looked at me and shook her head. "You can't get much worse."

The doctor kept saying, "I can't find out what's wrong with her." I told him I thought I knew what was wrong. "We'll have the tests back in a few minutes and then we'll know," he assured me.

I told him again I knew what was going on. "All right, what is it?" he asked me.

I'd been sitting around the hospital room for weeks and my legs had swollen up, so I took a Lasix fluid pill. "Maybe I'm having a reaction to that," I said.

"That's exactly what's wrong," said the doctor. The Lasix had drained all my fluids out and my electrolytes were all messed up.

I started feeling better and they took me back up to the suite. I wasn't going to tell John and June, but three or four days later a nurse slipped up and asked them how I was feeling.

Of course, June had to know all about it right away. "Honey, what was wrong with you?" she asked. "Why didn't you tell me?"

I told her I figured they had plenty of their own troubles.

Somebody else got a real scare one time when June was sick. We'd gotten word that a woman was coming to Nashville to kill June "because she'd messed up the Man in Black's life," whatever that meant. She said she was planning to sneak in and give June a shot to kill her.

Well, it wasn't long before a woman we didn't recognize came in with a syringe. Quick as anything John jumped up and knocked the tray out of her hand before we found out she really was one of June's nurses.

Then a little later Anita and I were in the sitting room when June started hollering. When I got to her room I saw a girl standing over June's bed. I grabbed the girl by the collar and slung her up against the wall. She was screeching and June was yelling and it was a while before we got it all straightened out. The woman said she was a songwriter and wanted June to listen to a tape. How she got in I'll never know. Later June told me, "Honey, I thought you were going to kill her."

By 2001 June was starting to be sick a lot. Every time, she thought that might be the end. "Oh, June, you're not going to die," I'd tell her. "My mother and sisters died young," she'd remind me sadly.

My heart would break every time she said, "I'll be in heaven with my mother and sisters soon." I think she knew it wouldn't be long.

The Last Days of June

JOHN AND JUNE had been staying at Mrs. Cash's house in the spring of 2003 while they installed an elevator at home. When I got to the house about six a.m. on April 28, John was waiting in his wheelchair. "Peggy, June's sick," he said. "Go see about her."

I went back to her bedroom. "June, are you okay?"

"I don't know, honey. I'm sicker than I've ever been," she said and asked me to take her to the hospital. She looked really bad.

I called Dr. Terri Jerkins and she told me bring her to the Emergency Room at Baptist.

June's bed was pretty high, but we used a footstool and I got her out of bed. She didn't even dress—we put a robe over her gown—or put on makeup. That's when I knew she was really sick.

I backed the Lincoln up to the garage and went to get her. June kissed John goodbye, and as we left the house she turned around in the door. "You've got to let me go this time," she told John. He just hung his head. I think June knew she wouldn't be back.

She looked like she was going to be sick. I had a wet washrag in a plastic bag for her. On the way she reached over and grabbed my hand.

"Honey, I'm so sick. Peggy, I don't think I'm going to make it," she said. The traffic was so bad–it was Monday morning at rush hour–that I thought we'd never make it to the hospital.

At Baptist we went straight to the Emergency Room. They let me stay with her until they admitted her to Intensive Care and started running tests. She was hurting really bad up under her ribs, and the doctor said it was gallstones. Then more tests showed she had fluid around her heart and her lungs.

The cardiologist came in to talk to her. "June, you've got a problem with your heart," he said. "A valve is completely gone; it's closed." He said it needed replacing right away.

"You mean heart surgery?" June asked him. "I don't think I want to do it."

"You have to," the doctor told her. "You think about this."

She thought about it for four or five days.

I'd sit with her for two or three hours at a time, leave for a bit and come back. I'd been in that hospital with her and John so many times they all knew who I was and they let me take care of her. I'd bathe her, put her makeup on, get her water–whatever she wanted.

For a while she was distracted by the air vent over the door. "Look at all the dirt in that vent," she said. "That's the filthiest thing I've ever seen." I put a wet towel on the end of an extra IV pole and poked at the vent. When I pulled that towel down it was just black. "Here I am, can hardly breathe, and I'm breathing all that dirt," June said.

As bad as she felt, she had me get out her makeup bag every morning to fix her hair and get her makeup on: eyeliner, lipstick, everything. "I have to do this for John. I have to get fixed up before he gets here or I'll look like a snake," she'd say.

John came to visit her almost every day, stayed about half an hour. He just kept saying "Babe"–that's what he always called her–"you're going to be all right, you're going to be all right." She warned him, "John, I'm really sick this time."

She asked him what he thought she should do about the operation. "Honey, I can't tell you. It's your body and you should make the decision," he said.

She finally decided to have the valve replaced. We waited around forever before the doctor came in and told us the surgery went fine and June was going to be okay. John Carter, Rosanne, and Kathy and Jimmy went on home.

They moved her out of Recovery and back to Intensive Care, where they took her off the respirator. That night John told her, "June, you're doing so good I'll get Betty to take me back home."

She was so weak she couldn't talk much. She raised up

her oxygen mask and threw kisses across the room to John.

June was really wrung out. "Honey, do you think you could get me some ice chips?" she asked. I fed her ice chips with a spoon for nearly two hours. "That tastes so good," she sighed.

About eight-thirty that night she told me, "Honey, you look tired. Go lie down." Here she was after heart surgery worrying about me! "I'm fine, June," I told her.

She smiled at me. "You've always said you're fine. You never say 'no' to me or John. Now go." As I left she said–just like Maybelle always did–"Goodnight, honey. I love you."

I did go lie down until the nurse called me about eleven o'clock. June was having breathing problems. She said she was smothering. But after a while she got to feeling better and told me to go back to bed. "I'll have the nurses call you if I need you. We know where you're at."

About two a.m. I heard them call Code Blue to Intensive Care. I had a feeling something was really wrong. The nurse called me again and told me to get down there quick. "June is bad," she said. "You need to get John out here." I called Betty to go after John. "Don't let him know how bad she is," I said.

As I walked in the room I could hear her gasping for breath. It was really loud on the quiet floor.

They put her back on the respirator, but the doctor told me she was pretty bad. "She's been out twenty minutes. One minute is all it takes for the brain to stop functioning." I walked to the foot of the bed. I could tell by her eyes she was gone. Her body was still alive, but June had passed over.

John went back and forth between the house and the hospital for the next five days, staying as long as he could. He sat beside the bed and held June's hand. He wasn't in very good shape.

"I hate to see her lying there like that," he told me.

He made the decision to let June go. I remembered what she'd said as she left the house for the last time. I know John did, too.

It was hard for him to make up his mind, but he finally said she'd suffered enough. So on May 15 he kissed her goodbye and they unplugged her. John, John Carter, Cindy, Kathy, and I were there beside her. John was holding her hand. "Peggy, get her other hand," he said. At 4:52 p.m. on May 15, she was gone.

Betty and I took John up to his room. He was saying over and over, "We're going to make it, you and me and Betty," trying to reassure himself, I think. "We'll go to Virginia; we'll go to Jamaica. We'll make it," he said.

We stayed until the funeral home came for her at two in the morning. June and I had arrived at the hospital together eighteen days before, and we left together, her in the hearse and me following in the car. I felt as empty and lonely on that drive back to Hendersonville as I've ever felt in my life.

I had lost my best friend. And now John needed me even more.

* * *

The office made the arrangements with Hendersonville Funeral Home, where visitation was held. June's funeral was held May 18 at First Baptist Church of Hendersonville.

June lay in a pretty blue casket, her favorite color, surrounded by more than five hundred arrangements of the flowers she loved so much. John's manager Lou Robin had suggested asking for donations instead of flowers. But John said, "I'll make that decision. June loved flowers—let her have all the flowers she can get."

Carlene, Rosey, John Carter, and all John's girls except Cindy were there. Kris Kristofferson, Hank Jr., Rodney Crowell, Trisha Yearwood, Marty Stuart and Connie Smith were there. The Gatlin Brothers, the Oak Ridge Boys, Sheryl Crow, and Emmylou Harris sang gospel songs.

John was pretty upset at the service. He had told me several times he didn't want any of the children helping him. "I don't want anybody but you and Betty to push me in the wheelchair," he told me. He told us to sit beside him in the front row. "When it's time, I want you to help me walk up to the casket."

Between us we got him up there. He leaned over and kissed her, stood there for a few minutes. "Goodbye, sweetheart. I love you," he told her. Hearing that nearly broke my aching heart.

Family and friends came by the house after the funeral. The kids were there, along with some of June's "babies" and other friends—Hank Jr., Connie and Marty,

Sheryl Crow, Emmylou, and Larry Gatlin. It was pretty quiet. I stayed busy putting out the mountains of food everyone had sent.

After a while I got John in a golf cart and we all went up to the Bell Garden. John and June had collected bells from all over the world, big ones and little bitty ones. They hung a bell for every family member by the rose garden. They rang those bells for every birth, every death in the family.

We gathered around—the kids and grandkids, and John's good friends—while John rang June's bell seventy-three times in honor of the number of years June had on this Earth. What an awesome sound.

She would have been seventy-four on her next birthday, a little over a month from then.

The next day Betty and I took John to June's grave at Hendersonville Memory Gardens. He had told us again he didn't want anybody but us pushing him around. We drove as close as we could get, then put John in a golf cart to take him to the gravesite where June rested near Maybelle, Mr. Carter, Helen, and Anita.

"Babe, I'm here," he said to her, the same thing he always said when he got home.

The day after that, they finally finished installing the elevator and we moved back to the house. It was hard on all of us going back there.

John called out, "Babe, I'm here." But the house was silent.

John cried a lot; he didn't do much talking. He wasn't

eating. He told me, "The only thing that would hurt me now is if something happened to John Carter."

It wasn't all sad. Three or four days after the funeral he said, "You girls want to go fishing?"

John loved to go fishing. He always kept a carton of nightcrawlers in his office refrigerator. When I'd go shopping I'd ask him, "John, have you got worms?" He always laughed and said, "Yeah, I've got worms but I'm still going fishing."

Anyway, I gathered up our gear and loaded everything in the Jeep. On the way he told me how much he missed June. "But we're going to make it," he promised me.

At the pond we parked him on the bank with a pole. After a while he got hungry and I gave him a baloney and

John spent a lot of time after June died recording with producer Rick Rubin.

onion sandwich. In a minute he said, "Peggy, come here quick." He had his sandwich in one hand and a fish on the line in the other hand. I grabbed the sandwich and he pulled in a six-pound catfish. Going fishing was good for both of us that day.

During that time producer Rick Rubin had moved some equipment in and John did some recording. After a couple of sessions we headed back to the hospital again, this time for an asthma attack. He was released at noon and was back recording by one o'clock. Making music gave him something to focus on. It seemed to cheer him up.

It didn't last. June had a huge bathroom where she kept what she called "all my stuff": treasures like jewelry boxes, small vases, knick-knacks she had picked up, and pictures of the kids. John would go in there and sit, just looking at her stuff, holding her picture. We'd hear him talking to her. "I miss you, Babe. I'll see you soon," he said.

I think he just didn't have the will to live without June. In a few months he would lie beside her once more.

But I wouldn't be there to see him go. It was a time of change, and things changed quickly at the House of Cash.

Out On My Ear

FOR MANY YEARS we had returned to the Carter Fold in Hiltons, Virginia, to celebrate June's birthday on June 23. John was determined to continue the tradition.

His doctor said he was well enough to travel, but she arranged for a nurse to come every day to check his blood pressure and sugar level.

I drove him up there, with Betty and Anna following in the truck. We stopped by the roadside every time he had to pee. He didn't want to go into a public place, so we just pulled off onto the shoulder and helped him out. I laughed to think of all those people driving by never knowing Johnny Cash was peeing beside the road!

We visited with friends and relatives and celebrated Janette Carter's eightieth birthday. John made a couple of appearances at the Carter Fold, singing from his wheelchair—it was his last public performance. But he was feeling better and even got to where he could walk a few steps.

John Carter and his family came up to stay for a few days. That's where it all started.

I was sitting in the living room talking to John when John Carter came in. Out of the clear blue sky he said, "Peggy, from now on I'm your boss and you'll answer to me." He turned to Betty and said, "That goes for you, too."

John looked shocked, but he just sat there like a mummy. I said, "John Carter, I don't think so. If I thought for one minute that you were my boss, I would walk back to Nashville right now!" Betty got mad and said, "Let's pack our bags and go."

John Carter followed us upstairs, where we were throwing clothes in suitcases. "You can't leave my daddy," he said. "You're acting like children."

I went to tell John we were heading home, John said, "Honey, I'm sorry for what John Carter said. We've been invaded, but they won't be here long. You girls can't leave me."

He was right.

We stayed a few more days and then headed back home on July 6. All the way back, John kept saying, "We sure miss June, don't we?" He never said a word about John Carter's doings.

Back home I went to John and told him I'd like to take a few days off. It had been a pretty rough stretch, and I just needed some time for myself.

He told me, "Go on, you deserve it. I've got the nurses and Betty and I'll be fine."

Generous as always, he insisted on giving me some money for my trip. He handed me about two hundred dollars, all he had in his pocket. "If you need more, you have my credit card," he told me.

I went up to Kentucky to visit some friends. I took off for six days, the first time I'd been away from John and June for any length of time in I don't know how long.

Everything changed while I was gone. When I got back Betty warned me John Carter had been worrying his dad about me.

I went to work as usual on Monday, July 21. The nurse and a sitter were there, and so were John Carter and Cindy. John called me into his office. I sat down on the half-bed where he sometimes took a nap.

"Honey, did you have a good time?" he asked. But something else was on his mind. He asked me to shut the door.

He hung his head down. I could see something was hurting him. His voice sounded weak, and he had trouble getting the words out. "Peggy, because of your lack of respect for me and my family, I have to let you go," he said. "I can't work with you any longer."

He wouldn't look at me, just stared at the floor. I knew those were John Carter's words in his father's mouth; Betty had told me John Carter had been saying that the whole week I was gone.

Later one of the sitters told me the same thing. John Carter hassled his dad all week to get rid of me, staying on his back the whole time. She told me what she'd heard.

"Daddy, she has no respect for you," John Carter had said.

"Son, you know that's not true," John had protested.

"Oh, yes, it is, Daddy, and you need to get rid of her," he said.

"I can't get rid of Peggy. She's been too faithful for thirty-three years," the sitter had heard John say. But he was too weak to fight for long.

"Son, you're making me sick," he told John Carter. "I don't need this." At one point, the nurse told me, John even ordered his son out of the house.

But in the end John Carter got what he wanted.

John was saying, "You can either resign–"

I interrupted him. "I can't believe this," I said. In thirty-three years we'd never had a problem; neither he nor June had ever criticized me or raised their voice to me. John had even given me a big raise just a few weeks before.

But I wasn't surprised. I knew John was too sick to fight about it.

He started again. "You can either resign–"

"I do have respect for you," I insisted. "I *do* have respect for you."

"You can either resign or you're fired," he finished, still without looking up. "Karen has some papers for you to sign."

Stunned, I could only say "Okay, John." I left, but I told Karen, his financial manager, that I wouldn't sign a damn thing.

I went out with my head up. I kept my cool until I got to my Jeep, but I cried all the way home.

The Bitter End

I CRIED OFF AND on for weeks.

I cried for June.

She'd always said I was like a sister to her. She even wrote that in the front of one of her books and gave it to me. She made me feel like part of her family.

I thought about a time a couple of months before she died. I'd brought her and John up some supper, and June insisted I sit and eat with them. June said, "Me and John just got to talking and we don't know what we'd do without you. We never could do better than what you've done for us."

I cried for John.

June had always told me, "Honey, you can do anything." I'd shown her that over the years: I could fix the roof, paint the house, put up curtains, mow the yard, drive the tour bus, cook for two hundred people at a moment's notice, be there every time she or Maybelle or John wanted something. Everything but iron clothes and fix hair, I always joked.

But, sadly, in the end what I couldn't do was be with John in his last days.

All the people taking care of him now were strangers. I know how much he hated undressing in front of them, letting them bathe him, needing help to go to the bathroom. I can hear him saying, "I don't want everybody seeing my behind." Even when he had round-the-clock care, John had always wanted me or Betty give him a bath.

It just killed me knowing I couldn't be there for him. This couldn't have been what he wanted. When your time's getting near, you need people you love, people who love you, close at hand.

I know John wouldn't have fired me if he hadn't been so sick and so sad about June. I know he thought that I would be taking care of him for the rest of his life. I sure did.

It hadn't been a year since we'd been talking on the porch in Jamaica. He and June wanted to give me a big party on my sixtieth birthday. I told them to wait a couple of years and make it a retirement party.

"Peggy, you can't retire until me and June are gone," John had said.

"Well, how long are you going to live?" I asked him right back. They both got tickled at that.

I believe with all my heart that John just gave up when June died and he was waiting out his time.

I cried for myself.

Here I was all alone in my own house that I'd hardly ever been to. I'd never even unpacked all my boxes. I was lonely. After all, I had spent a lot of years with famous people and their famous friends and traveled all over the world. And suddenly the job I'd spent more than half my life on was taken away. After thirty-three years of taking care of Maybelle, June, and John, I was finished. The only one I had to take care of now was me.

A little over six weeks later, I woke up in the middle of the night, something I hardly ever do. I was sitting on the side of the bed eating peanut butter crackers and drinking a Coke when the phone rang. It was Lorrie Bennett, Anita Carter's daughter. I knew, but I asked her anway. "Lorrie, what's wrong?"

"Peggy, Uncle John just died."

I was just numb, but I was glad he was finally at peace . . . and reunited with June.

That was September 12. The funeral was three days later. Nobody, including John Carter, was going to keep me from going.

All alone, I walked down the aisle to the casket and told John goodbye.

So Sad and Alone

I STILL WONDER WHY it had to end this way.

But I keep remembering something June always told me. "God will take care of you no matter what," she'd say. "Honey, put it in God's hands."

So I have. I'm at peace with what happened. And I've got thirty-six years of memories with the Carter and Cash families that no one can take away from me.

I go to the cemetery at least once a week. Every time I drive by I can't help but stop and spend ten or fifteen minutes just talking with John and June and Maybelle. It's awful hard to let go of people you've loved so much, people you've been so close to, people you've seen at their best and at their worst, for so many years.

I know I can't bring them back.

But I can let the world know the Maybelle, June, and John that I knew and loved, so you can love them too.

Other books by Peggy Knight

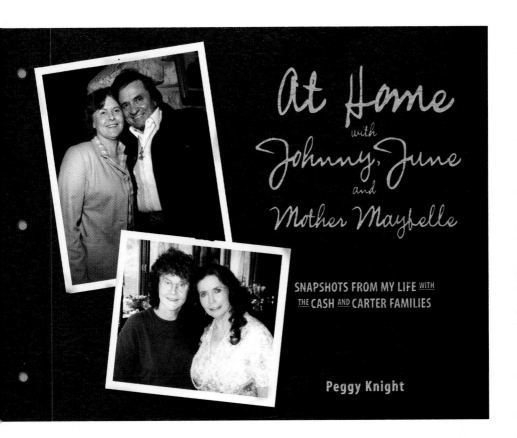

At Home with Johnny, June and Mother Maybelle
2004

Other books by Peggy Knight

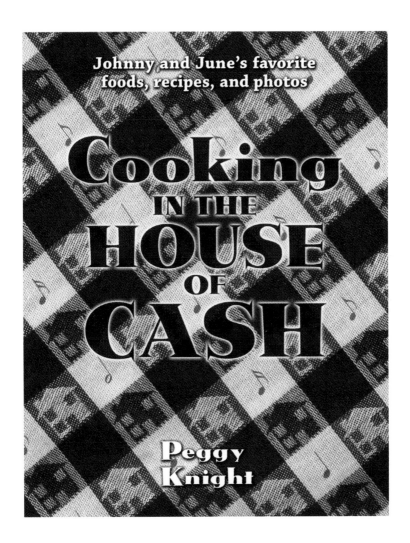

Cooking in the House of Cash
2004